10

MINUTE GUIDE TO

WINDOWS 95

SECOND EDITION

by Sue Plumley

A Division of Macmillan Computer Publishing
201 West 103rd St., Indianapolis, Indiana 46290 USA

For Hugh Bender

©1997 by Que® Corporation

Library of Congress Catalog Card Number: 97-65011

International Standard Book Number: 0-7897-1160-5

99 98 97   8 7 6 5 4 3 2 1

Interpretation of the printing code: the rightmost double-digit number is the year of the book's first printing; the rightmost single-digit number is the number of the book's printing. For example, a printing code of 97-1 shows that this copy of the book was printed during the first printing of the book in 1997.

Printed in the United States of America

Publisher Roland Elgey

Publishing Director Lynn E. Zingraf

Editorial Services Director Elizabeth Keaffaber

Managing Editor Michael Cunningham

Director of Marketing Lynn E. Zingraf

Acquisitions Editor Martha O'Sullivan

Technical Specialist Nadeem Muhammed

Product Development Specialist Henly Wolin

Technical Editor Rick Brown

Production Editor Tom Lamoureux

Copy Editors Nick Zafran, Kate Givens, Elizabeth A. Barrett

Book Designer Barbara Kordesh

Cover Designer Dan Armstrong

Production Team Malinda Kuhn, Mary Hunt, Daniela Raderstorf, Beth Rago

Indexer Tim Wright

We'd Like to Hear from You!

As part of our continuing effort to produce books of the highest possible quality, Que would like to hear your comments. To stay competitive, we *really* want you, as a computer book reader and user, to let us know what you like or dislike most about this book or other Que products.

You can mail comments, ideas, or suggestions for improving future editions to the address below, or send us a fax at 317-581-4663. For the online inclined, Macmillan Computer Publishing has a forum on CompuServe (type **GO QUEBOOKS** at any prompt) through which our staff and authors are available for questions and comments. The address of our Internet site is **http://www.mcp.com/que** (World Wide Web).

In addition to exploring our forum, please feel free to contact me personally to discuss your opinions of this book: I'm **[hwolin@aol.com]** on America Online, and I'm **[hwolin@mcp.com]** on the Internet.

Although we cannot provide general technical support, we're happy to help you resolve problems you encounter related to our books, disks, or other products. If you need such assistance, please contact our Tech Support department at 800-545-5914 ext. 3833.

To order other Que or Macmillan Computer Publishing books or products, please call our Customer Service department at 800-835-3202 ext. 666.

Thanks in advance—your comments will help us to continue publishing the best books available on computer topics in today's market.

Henly Wolin
Product Development Specialist
Que Corporation
201 W. 103rd Street
Indianapolis, Indiana 46290
USA

CONTENTS

INTRODUCTION

Windows 95 provides a powerful yet easy-to-use operating system that enables you to use a variety of applications in addition to connecting to a variety of networks. The features and procedures of Windows 95 are similar to those of 3.11, but with more power, utility, and flexibility.

THE WHAT AND WHY OF WINDOWS 95

Windows 95 is an exceptional operating system that enables you to perform tasks—such as opening programs, copying files, editing documents, and so on—that help you get your work done quickly and easily. In addition, Windows 95 lets you connect to your company's network to access other computers, files, and printers as well as to the Internet, for an entire world of possibilities.

Windows 95 is a graphical user interface (GUI), which means that Windows provides a workspace that is graphical, and therefore, easy to use and understand. As you become familiar with Windows 95, you'll find that it makes it easy-to-use applications effectively to complete your work and manage your files.

 Graphical User Interface   A GUI (pronounced "gooey") makes interacting with your computer easy. You usually use a mouse to point at and select icons (small pictures that often represent files or application programs), and you choose operations (commands from menus) to perform. A GUI is an alternative to a command-line interface such as DOS, where the user enters text commands from a keyboard.

Why use Windows 95? Windows makes using your computer faster and easier in the following ways:

- You can work in and have several applications open on-screen at the same time, if you like. You also can easily switch between open applications and share data between them, which saves you time and effort.

- The graphical user interface is easy to understand and use, so you'll be up and running quickly. Once you get started, you'll be surprised at how quickly your educated guesses become correct ones.

- All application programs designed for Windows 95 look similar: title bars, menus, icons, even commands are often comparable. In addition, Windows applications use similar keyboard and mouse operations to select objects and choose commands. To a great extent, once you've learned one application, you've learned a part of them all.

- With Windows 95, you can integrate a variety of servers, including Windows NT, NetWare, TCP/IP, Microsoft LAN Manager, among others.

- You can use both 16-bit and 32-bit applications.

- Video and graphics applications run smoothly so that multimedia applications, games, and graphics programs such as CorelDRAW! really shine.

Windows 95's GUI provides a common approach to using a variety of applications for your computer. Learning Windows is fast, easy, and fun—and it takes a minimum of effort.

WHY THE *10 MINUTE GUIDE TO WINDOWS 95*?

The *10 Minute Guide to Windows 95* can save even more of your precious time. Each lesson is designed so that you can complete it in 10 minutes or less, so you'll be up-to-speed in basic Windows 95 skills quickly.

Although you can jump between lessons, starting at the beginning is a good plan. The bare-bones basics are covered first, and more advanced topics are covered later.

CONVENTIONS USED IN THIS BOOK

To help you move through the lessons easily, I've used the following conventions:

What you type	Information you type appears in bold color type.
Items you select	Commands, options, and icons you select as well as keys you press appear in color type.

In telling you to choose menu commands, this book uses the format *menu name, menu command*. For example, if I say "choose File, Properties," you are to open the File menu and select the Properties command.

In addition to these conventions, the *10 Minute Guide to Windows 95* uses the following icons to identify helpful information:

Plain English tips define new terms or terms that may be unfamiliar to you, such as technical terminology, jargon, and so on.

Timesaver Tips include keyboard and mouse shortcuts and hints that can save you time and energy.

Panic Button icons identify areas where new users often run into trouble, and offer practical solutions to those problems.

ACKNOWLEDGMENTS

I'd like to thank all of the people at Que who were involved with this project. First and foremost, all my gratitude to Martha O'Sullivan for her support and friendship. Martha, you're the best! Thanks too, to Henly Wolin and Tom Lamoureux for your hard work and advice. And thanks to the Que team of copy and tech editors, production people, indexers, and everyone else who makes a book successful.

TRADEMARKS

All terms mentioned in this book that are known to be trademarks have been appropriately capitalized. Que cannot attest to the accuracy of this information. Use of a term in this book should not be regarded as affecting the validity of any trademark or service mark.

Navigating the Windows 95 Desktop

In this lesson, you learn to start and shut down Windows, how to work with the parts of the Windows desktop, and how to use a mouse to manipulate items on the desktop.

Starting Windows 95

To start Windows 95, you simply turn on your computer and monitor. As your computer *boots*, Windows loads the files it needs to run. You'll notice the Windows 95 logo screen and several black screens with white type.

After the operating system is loaded, a password dialog box appears asking for your *user name* and your *password*. If you are a member of a network, you must use the exact user name and password assigned to you by your network administrator; if you are not sure of what to enter in this dialog box, ask your administrator. You should use the same user name and password each time you *log on* to Windows so that your desktop, applications, and customization settings will always be the same. By default, Windows displays the log on dialog box if you're on a network. If you don't see a log on dialog box, you don't have to enter a user name or password to work in Windows.

Boot   A term used to describe a computer's starting up process, during which the operating system and configuration files are loaded into the computer's memory.

User Name and Password   Identifies you to your computer or to the network server, and protects your computer from illegal entry.

Log On   Attaching to the network so you can use its resources—files, printers, and so on.

Follow these steps to open the Windows program if you're on a network:

1. Enter the following information:

   User Name   The name by which you are identified to your computer or the network.

   Password   Your personal watchword for logging in to the computer or network.

2. Press Enter to start Windows.

Error Message!   Many different errors could occur at this point. For example, a message might appear on your screen telling you a connection could not be restored or that you're not a valid user. First, make sure you've typed your password correctly and have used the appropriate case when typing. If you have a problem connecting to the network, see your network administrator for help.

TIP

Should I Press Enter or Click OK?   Pressing Enter in a dialog or message box is the same as choosing the OK button; pressing the Escape key is the same as choosing the Cancel button.

UNDERSTANDING THE WINDOWS DESKTOP

After Windows appears, you will see various items on the screen, as shown in Figure 1.1. The items you see enable you to open applications, manage files, send and receive mail, and perform many other tasks throughout your day. Depending on your installation, you may or may not see all of the items shown in the following figure.

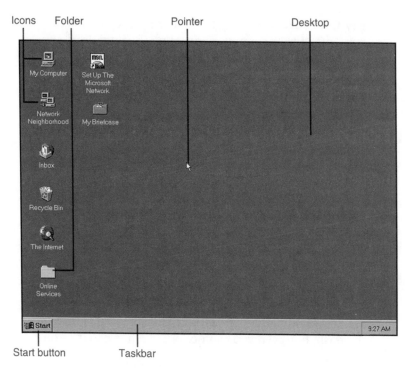

FIGURE 1.1   Common components of the Windows screen.

The components of the Windows screen include:

- **Desktop**   This is the background on which all other
  elements appear. You can think of the Windows desktop
  like the top of your own traditional office desk. Just as
  you can move papers around, hide certain items in draw-
  ers, and add and remove things on your desk, you can
  manipulate things on your Windows desktop.

- **Icons**   Icons are pictures that represent programs (the
  Internet, Word for Windows, Excel, and so on), folders,
  files, printer information, computer information, and so
  on, in both Windows 95 and Windows applications. Most
  often, you use icons to open folders and files.

- **My Computer**   The My Computer icon represents the contents of your computer, including the hard drive, floppy and CD-ROM drives, applications, folders, files, and so on. Double-click an icon to open it and view its contents.

- **Network Neighborhood**   This icon displays other computers connected to your computer on a Microsoft or other type of network, such as NT or NetWare.

- **Inbox**   The Inbox represents Microsoft Exchange, a program you can use to fax and e-mail other computers.

- **The Internet**   If you have access to an Internet Service Provider, you can use the Internet Explorer to access the Net, including Web pages and e-mail.

- **Recycle Bin**   The Recycle Bin is a place in which deleted objects remain until you empty the trash. You can retrieve items—files, programs, pictures, and so on—from the Recycle Bin after you delete them. Once you empty the trash, however, you can no longer retrieve items from the bin.

- **My Briefcase**   My Briefcase is a feature you can use for copying and transferring files from your computer to a notebook or other computer. My Briefcase enables you to easily transfer and update your files.

- **Online Services**   This folder icon enables you to quickly and easily sign up for any of the online services it contains, including America Online, AT&T WorldNet, and CompuServe. You must have a modem connected to your computer and configured before using one of these services.

- **Set Up The Microsoft Network**   A step-by-step guide to configuring your computer and connecting to Microsoft's special Internet network. Again, you'll need a modem to use this feature.

- **Taskbar**   The Taskbar contains the Start button, any open application or window buttons, and the time. You can click a taskbar button to open the window or application it represents. Use the Start button to open programs, documents, help, and so on.

- **Start Button**   The Start button displays a menu from which you can choose to open an application, open a document, customize Windows, find a file or folder, get help, or shut down the Windows 95 program.

- **Folder**   A folder contains files, programs, or other folders on your computer; for example, the Online Services folder contains programs that let you sign up for an online service such as CompuServe. A folder is the same thing as a directory.

- **Pointer**   The pointer is an on-screen icon (usually an arrow) that represents your mouse, trackball, touchpad, or other selecting device. You use it to select items and choose commands. You move the pointer by moving the mouse or other device across your desk or mouse pad. You'll learn how to use the mouse in the next section.

USING THE MOUSE

You use the mouse to perform many actions in Windows and in Windows applications. With the mouse, you can easily select an icon, folder, or window, among other things. Selecting involves two steps: pointing and clicking. You also can open icons and folders by double-clicking them, and you can move an item by clicking and dragging that particular object.

To *point* to an object (icon, taskbar, Start button, and so on) move the mouse across your desk or mouse pad until the on-screen mouse pointer touches the object. You can pick up the mouse and reposition it if you run out of room on your desk. To *click*, point the mouse pointer at the object you want to select, and then press and release the left mouse button. If the object is an icon or window, it becomes highlighted. When following steps in this book, click the left mouse button unless the directions specify otherwise.

The right mouse button can be used when you want to display a shortcut, or a quick menu. To *right-click*, point the mouse pointer at an object—folder, taskbar, desktop, and so on—and click the right mouse button. A shortcut menu that presents common commands relating to the object appears. If, for example, you right-click a folder, the menu might offer these commands: Open, Explore, Create Shortcut, and Properties. The items that appear on the menu depend on the object you're right-clicking.

When you *double-click* an item, you point to the item and press and release the left mouse button twice quickly. Double-clicking is often a shortcut to performing a task. For example, you can open a folder or window by double-clicking its icon.

You can use the mouse to move an object (usually a window, dialog box, or icon) to a new position on-screen. You do this by *clicking and dragging* the object. To drag an object to a new location on-screen, point to the object, press and hold the left mouse button, move the mouse to a new location, and release the mouse button. The object moves with the mouse cursor as you drag it. If you want some practice with the mouse, open the Solitaire game and play a round or two; choose Start, Programs, Accessories, Games, and then Solitaire.

You also can perform certain actions, such as selecting multiple items or copying items, by performing two additional mouse operations. *Shift+click* means to press and hold the Shift key and then click the left mouse button while pointing to various objects; *Ctrl+click* means to press and hold the Ctrl key, and then click the left mouse button. The result of either of these actions depends on where you are in Windows.

USING THE START BUTTON

The Windows Start button provides access to programs and documents, the help feature, find feature, and many other elements in Windows 95. You'll use the Start button to perform most tasks in Windows. For more information about using menus, see Lesson 3.

To use the Start button, follow these steps:

1. Point the mouse at the Start button, located on the taskbar, and click the button. The Start menu appears (see Figure 1.2). Your Start menu may display more options than the one in the figure, depending on what is installed to your computer.

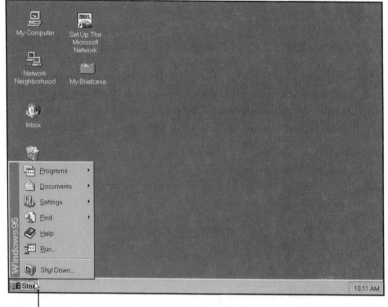

Click here to begin

FIGURE 1.2   The Start menu provides easy access to programs.

2. Click the task or command you want to display, as follows:

   • **Programs**   Displays a secondary, or cascading, menu that includes Windows Accessory programs, Online Services, the Internet Explorer, and other programs on your computer.

   • **Documents**   Displays up to 15 of the most recently opened documents; for quick and easy access, click the document name and the application. The document opens, ready to work.

- **Settings** Displays a secondary menu that includes the Control Panel and Printer folders, and the Taskbar command for customizing your Windows setup. For more information, see Lesson 24.

- **Find** Enables you to search for specific files, folders, or computers. You can search your own hard drive or the network drive.

- **Help** Displays help for performing tasks and procedures in windows. For more information, see Lesson 5.

- **Run** Enables you to enter a command line (such as a:\install) to run a program from a hard or floppy disk or a CD-ROM.

- **Shut Down** Displays the Shut Down dialog box in which you prepare your computer before turning it off.

Secondary or Cascading Menu An arrow after any menu command designates another menu, called a cascading or secondary menu. It will appear if you choose that command. Windows supplies as many as four cascading menus from the Start menu.

Using the Taskbar

In addition to the Start button, the taskbar displays buttons representing open windows and applications. You can quickly switch between open windows by clicking the button on the taskbar. Figure 1.3 shows the taskbar with two buttons: My Computer (representing the open My Computer window) and Exploring (representing the hidden, or minimized, Windows Explorer).

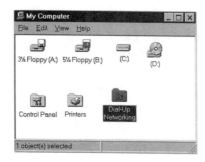

FIGURE 1.3 Open and minimized windows are represented on the taskbar by buttons and the window's name.

You can move the taskbar to the top, left, or right side of the screen to customize your workspace. Additionally, you can hide the taskbar until you need it.

To move the taskbar, click the mouse anywhere on the bar (except on a button) and drag the taskbar to the right, the left, or the top of the screen. As you drag, the taskbar relocates to that area. You can easily drag the taskbar back to the bottom if you prefer it there.

To hide the taskbar, follow these steps:

1. Click the Start button.

2. From the Start menu, click Settings and then click Taskbar. The sheet appears.

3. Choose the Auto Hide check box by clicking that box; then press Enter to close the dialog box. The taskbar slides off of the screen.

When you need the taskbar, move the mouse to where the taskbar was; you may have to slide the mouse off of the screen. The taskbar reappears.

Can't Display the Taskbar! If you move the mouse to where the taskbar should be and the taskbar doesn't display, press Ctrl+Esc to display the taskbar and open Start menu.

To show the taskbar all the time, click Start, Settings, Taskbar and click the Auto Hide check box so no check mark appears. Press Enter to close the dialog box.

SHUTTING DOWN WINDOWS 95

Before you turn off your computer, you must shut down Windows to ensure you don't lose any data or configuration. You also can shut down Windows and restart the computer to switch to MS-DOS mode, for example, or to log on to the network under a different name. Following are the Shut Down options available to you in the Shut Down Windows dialog box:

- **Shut Down the Computer**   Choose this option when you're finished using your computer for the day. When Windows displays a message telling you to shut off your computer, you can safely turn off the machine.

- **Restart the Computer**   Choose this option to shut down and then restart the computer in Windows mode. You'll use this option when you've changed configuration in the Control Panel, for example, and you want that configuration to take effect.

- **Restart the Computer in MS-DOS Mode**   This option shuts down Windows and starts the computer back in DOS mode, with a black screen, white type, and a C-prompt, or command prompt. From the command prompt, you can enter many familiar DOS commands or install DOS applications. See Lesson 17 for more information.

- **Close All Programs and Log On as a Different User**   Choose this option when you're sharing a computer with someone and they are already logged on to the network. When you choose this option, the network logon dialog box appears in which you can enter your user name and password.

To shut down Windows, follow these steps:

1. From the Desktop, click Start, Shut Down.

2. When the Shut Down Windows dialog box appears, choose one of the options previously described. To quit working on the computer, choose Shut Down the Computer. Then choose Yes.

3. Do not turn the computer off until Windows displays the message telling you that it's okay to turn off your computer.

In this lesson, you learned to start and shut down Windows, work with the parts of the Windows desktop, and use a mouse to manipulate items on the desktop. In the next lesson, you learn to work with windows.

2 WORKING WITH A WINDOW

In this lesson, you learn to open, resize, move, view, close a window, and how to use scroll bars to view more of a window.

WHAT IS A WINDOW?

A *window* is a boxed area in which you view files, folders, drives, hardware icons, or other elements. Figure 2.1 shows the components that make up a window. Many of these components are the same for all windows in Windows 95 and Windows applications, which makes it easy for you to manage your work. Keep in mind that although most windows are similar, you'll run across some windows that don't have all of the following components.

You can open and close a window, reduce and enlarge a window, and move a window around—which is what this lesson is all about. In addition, you can open more than one window at a time, stack one window on top of another, and otherwise manipulate windows as explained in Lesson 7. Table 2.1 briefly describes the common elements of a window.

TABLE 2.1 WINDOW ELEMENTS

ELEMENT	DESCRIPTION
Title bar	Contains the window's name, the Control menu, and the Minimize, Maximize or Restore, and the Close buttons.

ELEMENT	DESCRIPTION
Menu bar	Contains menus with related commands and options that help you control the window and its contents. See additional information about menus in Lesson 3.
Control menu button	Contains commands that help you manage the window itself.
Toolbar	Graphic tool buttons that represent shortcuts to various menu commands you use in your work.
Minimize button	A button that reduces the window to a button on the taskbar.
Maximize button	A button that enlarges the window to fill the screen.
Close button	A button that closes the window.
Folders	Icons within windows that represent directories; folders can hold other folders and files.
Files	Document, spreadsheet, database, program, and other components stored in folders on a drive in your computer.
Windows border	A rim around a restored window that you can use to resize the window.
Status bar	A bar across the bottom of the window that describes the contents of the window, such as free space, number of objects or files in a window, and so on.
Scroll bar	A vertical or horizontal bar that enables you to view hidden areas of a window.

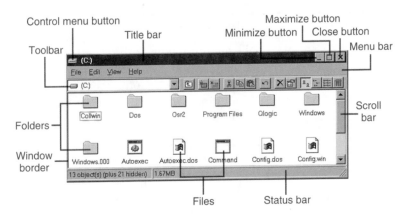

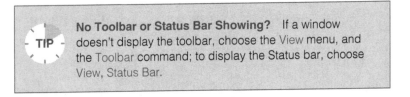

FIGURE 2.1 The elements of a typical window.

> **TIP** **No Toolbar or Status Bar Showing?** If a window
> doesn't display the toolbar, choose the View menu, and
> the Toolbar command; to display the Status bar, choose
> View, Status Bar.

WINDOWS CONTENTS

Windows 95 is made up of a series of windows that often contain
different items. When opened, each icon on your desktop, for
example, displays different contents just as various folders, files,
and applications display various contents. Additionally, after you
open a window, you can usually open items within the window,
such as icons, folders, programs, and documents. Often, you can
open a window within a window within a window, and so on,
until your desktop is filled with windows.

Following is an example of a set of windows you can open from
the My Computer icon:

- **My Computer window**   Displays hard drive icons, floppy disk and CD icons, Control Panel folder and the Printers folder; often this window also includes the Dial-Up Networking icon.

- **Hard drive icon**   Displays all folders (or directories) on that drive, plus any files found on the root directory (usually C).

- **Program Files folder**   Displays folders representing programs included with Windows, such as the Accessories, Internet Explorer, Online Services, and so on.

- **Internet Explorer folder**   Includes the Internet Explorer program and files needed to run the program, plus several text files you can read to get more information about the Internet Explorer.

OPENING A WINDOW

To open a window from an icon, double-click the icon. For example, point at the My Computer icon and double-click. If you do it correctly, the My Computer icon opens into the My Computer window.

 Having Double-Click Trouble?   If you have trouble opening a window by double-clicking, you need to practice the double-click movement. You can also change the speed of the double-click to better suit your "trigger" finger; see Lesson 25.

There is another method you can use to open a window. Just point to the icon and right-click once, and a shortcut menu appears. Select Open from the menu to open the window.

Sizing a Window with Maximize, Minimize, and Restore

You may want to increase the size of a window to see its full contents, or you may want to decrease a window to a button on the taskbar in order to make room for other windows. One way to resize a window is to use the Maximize, Minimize, and Restore commands found on the Control Menu. If you use the mouse, you will use the Maximize, Minimize, and Restore buttons located at the right end of the window's title bar. The buttons and commands work as described here.

Select the Maximize button, or command, to enlarge the window. A maximized hard drive window, for example, fills your entire screen, thus hiding any of the desktop in the background. Clicking the Maximize button of a program, document, or other window enlarges that window to fill the screen.

Select the Minimize button, or command, to reduce the window to a button on the taskbar.

Select the Restore button, or command, to return a window to the size it was before it was maximized. (The Restore button and command are available only after a window has been maximized; the Restore button replaces the Maximize button in a maximized window.)

Figure 2.2 shows the hard drive window (opened from My Computer) maximized; it fills the entire desktop. At full size, the hard drive window's Restore button is available. When the window is at any other size, you see the Maximize button instead of the Restore button.

To maximize, minimize, or restore a window with the mouse, click the appropriate button in the title bar of the window. To maximize, minimize, or restore a window using the Control menu, follow these steps:

Hard drive's title

Minimize and
Restore buttons

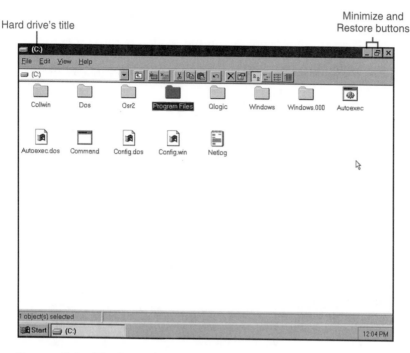

FIGURE 2.2   The hard drive window enlarges to fill the screen.

1. Click the Control menu button to open the window's
   Control menu; alternatively, press Alt+Spacebar.

2. Click the command (Restore, Minimize, or Maximize) you
   want to initiate. Alternatively, use the down arrow to
   move to and highlight the command, then press Enter.

SIZING A WINDOW'S BORDERS

At some point, you'll need a window to be a particular size to suit
your needs. For example, you might want to fit two or more windows on-screen at the same time. You can drag the window's
frame, or border, to change the size of the window. A window's
border appears only on a restored window, not on a maximized or
minimized window.

To use the mouse to size a window's borders, follow these steps:

1. Place the mouse pointer on the portion of the border that you want to resize: left or right side, top or bottom. When the mouse is positioned correctly, it changes shape to a double-headed arrow.

   Use the vertical double-headed arrow (on the top or bottom of the window border) to resize the window's height by dragging the frame up or down.

   Use the horizontal double-headed arrow (on the left or right window border) to resize the window's width by dragging the frame left or right.

   Use the diagonal double-headed arrow (on any of the four corners of the window border) to resize the window's height and width proportionally by dragging the corner diagonally.

2. Click and drag the border toward the center of the window to reduce the size of the window, or away from the center to enlarge the window.

3. When the border reaches the desired size, release the mouse button.

USING SCROLL BARS

Scroll bars appear along the bottom or the right edge of a window when the window contains more text, graphics, or icons than it can display.

Using scroll bars, you can move up, down, left, or right in a window. Figure 2.3 shows an example. Because all of the hard drive window's contents are not fully visible in the window, the scroll bars are present on the right side and the bottom of the window.

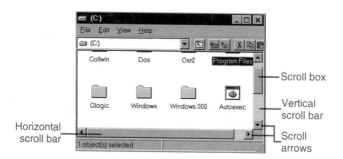

FIGURE 2.3   Use scroll bars to move within the window.

What Is a Scroll Bar?   A scroll bar is a bar that contains three items: two scroll arrows and a scroll box. You use the scroll arrows and the scroll box to move around in the window, scrolling a line at a time, or even a page at a time.

The following steps teach you how to use the scroll bars to view items not visible in the window:

1. To see an object that is down and to the right of the viewable area of the window, point at the down arrow located on the bottom of the vertical scroll bar.

2. Click the arrow, and the window's contents move up.

3. Click the scroll arrow on the right side of the horizontal scroll bar, and the window's contents shift to the left.

By its placement within the scroll bar, the scroll box depicts how much of a window is not visible. If you know approximately where something is in a window, you can drag the scroll box to get there quickly. To drag the scroll box and move quickly to a distant area of the window (top or bottom, left or right), use this technique:

1. Point to the scroll box in the scroll bar and press and hold the left mouse button.

2. Drag the scroll box to the new location.

3. Release the mouse button.

On the other hand, sometimes you may need to move slowly through a window (to scan for a particular icon, for example). You can move through the contents of a window one screen at a time by clicking inside the scroll bar on either side of the scroll box.

Empty Windows?   Don't worry if text, graphics, or icons don't appear in a window. Use the scroll bar to bring them into view. Items in any window appear first in the upper-left corner.

MOVING A WINDOW

When you start working with multiple windows, moving a window becomes as important as resizing one. For example, you may need to move one or more windows to make room for other work on your desktop, or you may need to move one window to see another window's contents. You can move a window easily with the mouse.

Don't Lose the Title Bar!   Be very careful that you do not move a window so far off the screen that you cannot see the title bar. If you lose the title bar, you may never be able to move the window back into full view.

To move a window, point at the window's title bar, press and hold the left mouse button, and drag the window to its new location.

VIEWING A WINDOW'S CONTENTS

Windows displays the contents of a window in icon form; for example, the elements in the My Computer window are represented by pictures of a hard drive, floppy drive, and folders. Other windows, such as your hard drive window, display elements as folders and files.

You can display the contents of any window in various ways so you can better see the contents. The default, or standard, view in most windows is by Large Icons (refer to Figure 2.3). Large icons help you quickly identify the contents. You also can view the contents of a window as follows:

- **Small Icons**   Contents are displayed with a small icon next to the file or folder name; small icons represent the application in which a file was created, a folder, or an executable program.

- **List**   Similar to small icons but the icons are even smaller.

- **Details**   Lists icon, file or folder name, file size, file type, and last date modified. When in Details view, you can click the heading button—Name, Size, Type, or Modified—to automatically sort the contents by that heading. For example, click Name and folders will list in alphabetical order followed by file names listed alphabetically.

Figure 2.4 shows four windows, each with a different view of the window's contents: Large Icons, Small Icons, Details, and List.

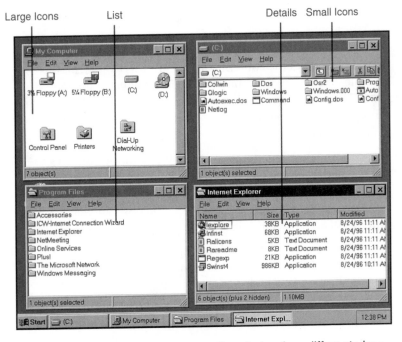

FIGURE 2.4   Display the contents of a window in a different view so you can easily identify files or folders.

To change views of the window's contents, choose View, and then select Large Icons, Small Icons, List, or Details.

CLOSING A WINDOW

When you're finished working with a window, you should close it. This often helps speed up Windows, conserve memory, and keeps your desktop from becoming cluttered.

To close a window, you can do any of the following:

- Click the Control menu button and choose Close.

- Click the Close button in the Title bar.

- Press Alt+F4.

- Choose File, Close.

- Double-click the window's Control menu button.

 Quickie Close   To quickly close several related open windows, hold the Shift key while clicking the Close button on the last window you opened.

In this lesson, you learned to open, resize, move, view, close a window, and how to use scroll bars to view more of a window. In the next lesson, you learn to use menus and toolbar buttons.

USING MENUS

In this lesson, you learn how to use toolbar buttons, select menus, open menus, choose menu commands, and use menu shortcuts.

USING TOOLBAR BUTTONS

Most windows and applications offer a toolbar containing various buttons you can use as shortcuts. Toolbar buttons represent common commands you often use in Windows, such as cut, copy, undo, and so on. The tools that are available to you depend on the window or application you're using. Figure 3.1 shows the toolbar for the My Computer window.

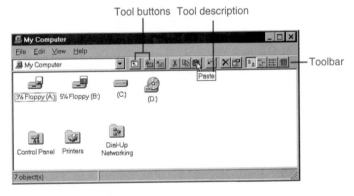

FIGURE 3.1 Use tool buttons to speed up your work.

 TIP **Handy Helpers** Most Windows applications provide helpful descriptors of the tools on a toolbar. Position the mouse pointer over any tool button and wait a second or two. A small box or bubble containing the button's name or a description of its function appears. When you move the mouse pointer, the description disappears. To activate the tool button, click it with the mouse.

To use a tool button, click it. Just like commands, any of a variety of results may occur. If, for example, you select a folder or file and choose the Copy tool button, a duplicate of the folder or file moves to the Windows Clipboard for pasting to another area later. If you choose the Undo tool button, the last action you performed is reversed.

WHAT IS A MENU?

A menu is a list of related commands that you use to perform tasks in Windows and in Windows applications (tasks such as copying or deleting selected items in a window). Menu commands are organized in logical groups. For example, all the commands related to arranging and opening windows are located on the Windows menu. The names of the available menus appear below the Title bar of any window or application that uses menus.

Lost with No Idea of What to Do?   Any time you're not sure what to do next or how to perform a specific task, click each menu in the application and read each command. Generally, you can find what you want in this way; if not, you can always choose the Help menu (described in Lesson 5).

In this book, I will use the format "menu title, menu command" to tell you to choose a command from a pull-down menu. For example, the sentence "choose File, Properties" means to "open the File menu and select the Properties command."

Pull-Down Menu   A menu that appears to "pull-down" from the menu bar. You access the menu by clicking its name in the menu bar. You then have several options to choose from within the pull-down menu.

CHOOSING MENU COMMANDS

To choose a menu command with the mouse, follow these steps:

1. Click the menu title in the menu bar. The menu opens to display the available commands.

2. To choose a particular command, simply click it. For example, to see the View commands available for the My Computer window, click the View menu in the menu bar. The View menu appears (see Figure 3.2).

Click here to display the menu

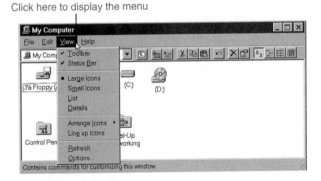

FIGURE 3.2 Click any menu to view its contents.

3. To make the menu disappear, click anywhere outside the menu.

To choose a command on the menu, move the mouse to that command and click. What happens next depends on the menu and the command.

TIP

Want to Use the Keyboard? If you want to use the keyboard to choose menu commands, press the Alt key to activate the menu bar of the active window. Use the left and right arrow keys to highlight the menu you want; then use the up and down arrows to highlight the command you want. Press Enter to activate the highlighted command. You could, alternatively, press Alt+ the underlined letter to activate a menu; press Alt+F, for example, to open the File menu and then press the underlined letter in the command you want to activate.

Reading a Menu

Windows menus contain a number of common elements that indicate what will happen when you choose a command, provide a shortcut, or limit your choice of commands. Some menus, for example, may contain commands that are dimmed or grayed-out. However, most commands perform some sort of task when you select them.

 Unavailable Commands If a command appears grayed-out, you cannot currently use that command. Grayed-out commands are only available for use under certain circumstances. For example, you cannot choose the Copy command or the Delete command if you have not first selected an object to copy or delete.

Depending on the type of command you select, one of four things will happen:

- An action will take place. For example, choosing File, Delete erases the selected icon or file.

- A dialog box will appear. Any command followed by an ellipsis (...) displays a dialog box containing related options (See Lesson 4 for more information).

- A secondary menu will appear. A command followed by an arrow displays a second (cascading) menu offering related commands.

- A feature will be turned on. A check mark or bullet appears to the left of the option on the menu and that option remains active until you either select a different bulleted option in the same menu or deselect the checked option by clicking it a second time.

TIP   **Separator Lines Give You a Clue** Commands on most menus are grouped together and divided by separator lines. When (bulleted) option commands are grouped, you can select only one option in the group, for example. When checked commands are grouped, you can choose as many or as few options as you want.

Figure 3.3 shows common menu elements: the ellipsis, the check mark, and the option bullets, an arrow with cascading menu, and separator lines.

To practice using menu commands, follow these steps:

1. In the My Computer window, choose View, Toolbar. The Toolbar displays, if it was not already displayed.

2. Choose View, Options (notice the ellipsis after the Option command). A dialog box appears.

3. To cancel the dialog box, choose Cancel.

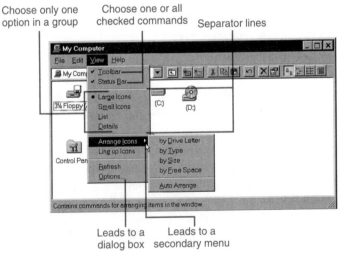

FIGURE 3.3 Indicators let you know what will happen before you select the command.

USING SHORTCUT KEYS INSTEAD OF MENUS

Until you become familiar with Windows and your various Windows applications, you'll need to use the menus to view and select commands. However, after you've worked in Windows for a while, you'll probably want to use shortcut keys for commands you use often. Shortcut keys enable you to select commands without using the menus. They generally combine the Alt, Ctrl, or Shift key with a letter key (such as W). If a shortcut key is available, it is listed on the pull-down menu to the right of the command.

For example, Figure 3.4 shows the Edit menu from the hard drive window on My Computer. As you can see, the shortcut key for Cut is **Ctrl+X**. You cannot use the shortcut key while the menu is open; you must either choose a command or cancel the menu. You can, however, remember the shortcut key and use it instead of opening the menu the next time you need to cut a file or folder.

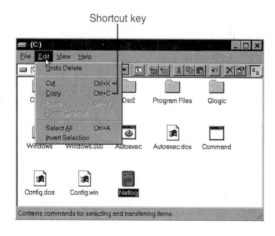

FIGURE 3.4 Use shortcut keys to save time.

USING SHORTCUT MENUS

Windows supplies a variety of shortcut, or quick, menus that contain common commands you often use. You can display a shortcut menu by right-clicking an object—the desktop, a window, a folder or file, and so on. The commands a shortcut menu displays depend on the item and its location.

To display and use a shortcut menu, point the mouse at the object you want to explore, cut, open, or otherwise manipulate, and right-click the mouse. The shortcut menu appears; move the mouse to the command and click again. Cancel a shortcut menu by clicking the mouse anywhere besides on the menu.

Figure 3.5 displays a shortcut menu resulting from right-clicking a hard drive icon.

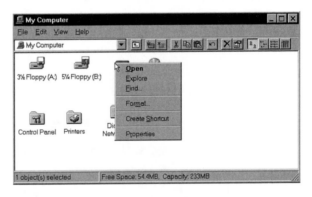

FIGURE 3.5   Quickly access a command with a right-click.

In this lesson, you learned how to use toolbar buttons, select menus, open menus, choose menu commands, and use menu shortcuts. In the next lesson, you learn to use dialog boxes.

USING DIALOG BOXES

In this lesson, you learn how to use the various dialog box components.

WHAT IS A DIALOG BOX?

Windows and Windows applications use dialog boxes to exchange information with you. As you learned in Lesson 3, a menu command followed by an ellipsis (...) indicates that a dialog box will appear. A dialog box asks for related information the program needs in order to complete the operation.

Windows also displays dialog boxes to give you information. For example, Windows might display a dialog box to warn you about a problem (as in "File already exists, Overwrite?") or to confirm that an operation should take place (to confirm you want to delete a file, for example).

Box Won't Go Away? If a dialog box won't go away and your computer beeps at you when you try to continue your work, don't worry. That beep is Windows' way of telling you that you must always respond to a dialog box before you can continue. You can press Enter or choose OK to accept the message or changes in the dialog box, or you can press the Esc key or choose Cancel to cancel the message or changes in the box.

USING THE COMPONENTS OF A DIALOG BOX

Dialog boxes vary in complexity depending on the program, the procedure, and the number of options in the actual box. Some simply ask you to confirm an operation before it is executed;

others ask you to choose, for example, a drive, folder, file name, file type, network path, or any of numerous other options.

The following list briefly explains the components of a dialog box. Not all dialog boxes contain all components, so don't be afraid to tackle a dialog box.

- **Text box**   A text box provides a place to type an entry, such as a file name, path (drive and directory), font, or measurement.

- **List box**   A list box presents a slate of possible options from which you can choose. Scroll bars often accompany a list box so you can view the items on the list. In addition, a text box is sometimes associated with a list box; you can either choose from the list or type the selection yourself.

- **Drop-down list box**   This box is a single-line list box with a drop-down arrow button to the right of it. When you click the arrow, the drop-down list box opens to display a list of choices. You can often scroll through a drop-down list as you do a list box.

- **Option buttons**   Option buttons present a group of related choices from which you can choose only one. Click the option button you want to select and all others become deselected.

- **Check box**   A check box enables you to turn an option on or off. You might find a single check box or a group of related check boxes. A check mark appears in the box next to any option that is active (turned on). In a group of check boxes, you can choose none, one, or any number of the options.

- **Command button**   When selected, a command button carries out the command displayed on the button (Open, Help, Quit, Cancel, or OK, for example). If there is an ellipsis on the button (as in Option...), choosing it will open another dialog box.

- **Tabs**   Tabs represent multiple sections, or pages, of a dialog box. Only one tab is displayed at a time, and each tab contains related options. Choosing a tab changes the options that appear in the dialog box.

USING TEXT BOXES

You use a text box to enter the information that Windows or a Windows application needs in order to complete a command. This information is usually a file name, folder name, measurement, style or font name, or other information related to the original menu and command. Figure 4.1 shows a text box and list boxes in the Open dialog box (accessed from the Windows WordPad File menu).

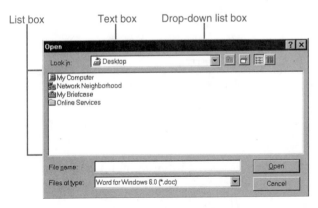

FIGURE 4.1   Use text boxes and list boxes to specify your preferences.

Save Time and Trouble If you want to replace text that's already in a text box, drag your mouse I-beam over the text (to highlight the text) and start typing. When you type the first character, the original text is deleted. Often when you first open a dialog box containing a text box, there is already text present and highlighted; if you start typing, you automatically delete the current text.

To activate a text box using the mouse, position the mouse over the text box (the mouse pointer changes to an I-beam) and click. The I-beam pointer shape indicates that the area you're pointing to will accept text. Look for the I-beam when you want to enter text in a dialog box. Notice that the insertion point (a flashing vertical line) appears in the active text box.

To activate a text box using the keyboard, press Alt+selection letter. (The selection letter is the underlined letter in a menu, command, or option name.) After you have activated a text box and typed text into it, you can use several keys to edit the text. Table 4.1 outlines these keys.

TABLE 4.1 EDITING KEYS FOR TEXT BOXES AND OTHER TEXT

KEY	DESCRIPTION
Delete	Deletes the character to the right of the insertion point
Backspace	Erases the character to the left of the insertion point
End	Moves the insertion point to the end of the line
Home	Moves the insertion point to the beginning of the line
Arrow keys	Moves the insertion point one character in the direction of the arrow

continues

TABLE 4.1   CONTINUED

KEY	DESCRIPTION
Shift+End	Selects the text from the insertion point to the end of the line
Shift+Home	Selects the text from the insertion point to the beginning of the line
Shift+Arrow key	Selects the next character in the direction of the arrow
Ctrl+C	Copies the selected text to the Clipboard
Ctrl+V	Pastes the selected text from the Clipboard

Clipboard   The Clipboard is a tool provided by Windows that holds any cut or copied text for you so you can paste it to another location, document, or application. For more information, see Lesson 8.

USING LIST BOXES

You use a list box to select from multiple available options. For example, you use the Look In list box in the Open dialog box (refer to Figure 4.1) to select the drive that contains the file you want to open.

To select an item from a list box using the mouse, click the appropriate list item and click OK. You can also select more than one item in many list boxes by holding the Shift key as you click. The item you select automatically appears in the linked box above the list box.

To select an item from a drop-down list box, open the list box by clicking the down-arrow, and then click the appropriate item.

USING OPTION BUTTONS

Option buttons enable you to make a single choice from a group of possible command options. For example, the Print Range options displayed in Figure 4.2 enable you to choose which pages of your document you want to print. The active option (the All option in Figure 4.2) has a filled-in circle. Figure 4.2 was created in WordPad using the **File**, **Print** command.

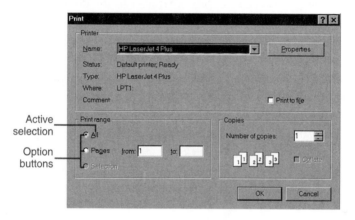

Active selection

Option buttons

FIGURE 4.2   You can choose only one option in a group.

To select an option button, click the circle for the option you want.

USING CHECK BOXES

For options that you can select (activate) or deselect (deactivate), Windows and Windows applications usually provide check boxes. When a check box is selected, an **X** or a check mark appears in the box, indicating the associated option is active (see Figure 4.3; this figure is from WordPad using the **Format**, **Font** command.)

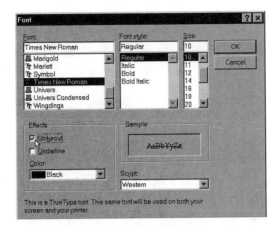

FIGURE 4.3   A check mark indicates the active, or selected option.

To select or deselect a check box, click the box.

USING COMMAND BUTTONS

You use command buttons to either accept or reject the changes you've made in a dialog box, to get help, or to access another related dialog box. To select a command button, simply click it.

Figure 4.4 shows the two most common command buttons: **OK** and **Cancel**. Select OK to accept the information you have entered or to verify an action and close the dialog box. Select Cancel to leave the dialog box without putting into effect the changes you made in the dialog box.

Quick and Easy   You can press the Enter key in a dialog box to quickly accept the changes and close the dialog box. Similarly, you can press the Esc key to cancel the changes made to the dialog box and close the box at the same time.

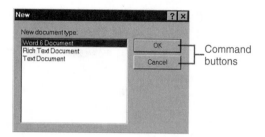

Figure 4.4   Use command buttons to control the dialog box.

 Accidents Happen   If you accidentally select Cancel in a dialog box, don't worry. You can always reenter the changes to the dialog box and continue. However, you need to be more careful when you select OK in a dialog box. The instructions you enter in the dialog box will be executed and changing them back may be harder than canceling changes.

 Close Means Cancel   Choosing the Close button in a dialog box is the same thing as canceling it.

Using Property Sheets and Tabs

As noted previously, property sheets are similar to dialog boxes in the components they contain: check boxes, list boxes, text boxes, command buttons, and so on. Figure 4.5 shows the Taskbar Properties sheet.

Tabs——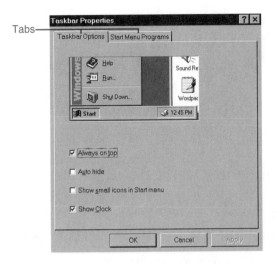

FIGURE 4.5   Choose a tab that represents the options you want to change.

In a property sheet containing more than one tab, choose options within the sheet and then click Apply to accept the changes. You can then select the other tabs and make other changes. Once you've chosen Apply, however, you cannot cancel those changes using Cancel; you must go back to the tab and change the options.

To select a tab, click the tab with the mouse pointer.

In this lesson, you learned how to use the various dialog box components. In the next lesson, you learn how to use Windows help.

5 LESSON

USING
WINDOWS 95
HELP

In this lesson, you learn how to get help, use the Help feature's shortcut buttons, and use the What's This? feature.

GETTING HELP IN WINDOWS 95

Windows offers several ways to get online help—instant on-screen help for menu commands, procedures, features, and other items. Online help is information that appears in its own window whenever you request it. Windows' Help feature offers three types of help: Index, Find, and Contents features.

The Contents feature displays a list of topics (such as Introducing Windows and Tips and Tricks) as well as a 10 minute tour of using Windows. The Index feature enables you to access specific categories of topics—such as adapters, disk configuration, copying, and so on. Find lets you search for specific words and phrases—such as About, Mem, Printing, and so on.

 TIP **Setting Up Help** The first time you choose Find in Windows Help, Windows runs a Find Setup Wizard that compiles every word from the Help files into a database you will use to find subjects. Follow the directions and the Wizard will guide you.

Fast Help   Most dialog boxes, including Help dialog boxes, include a Help button (a question mark in the title bar) that enables you to get help on items within the dialog box. Click the question mark and point the mouse at an area you have a question about. Windows displays a box with a definition or other information relating to your question. When you're finished reading the help, click the mouse to hide the information box.

USING THE CONTENTS FEATURE

You can get help with common procedures using Help's Contents feature. The Contents feature displays the top level groups of information covered in Help, such as How To and Troubleshooting. When you select a major group, a list of related topics appears, as shown in Figure 5.1.

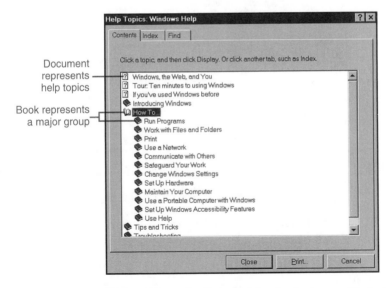

Document represents help topics

Book represents a major group

FIGURE 5.1   Choose from the listed topics for task-specific help.

Follow these steps to use Help's Contents feature:

1. Choose Start and then choose Help. The Help Topics: Windows Help dialog box appears; select the Contents tab if it is not already selected.

> **Pick a Tab** The last tab in the Help Topics window that you accessed is the one that appears the next time you open Help.

2. In the Contents list, double-click the book icon in front of the topic you want to view. The book opens and related topics appear either in a list of books or documents.

3. Double-click a document icon to view information about that topic (see Figure 5.2).

FIGURE 5.2 A Help window tells you what you need to know when you have trouble printing, for example.

4. When you finish with the Help topic, you can choose one of the following buttons:

   Close (X)   To close the Help window and return to the desktop.

   Help Topics   To return to the Contents tab of the Help Topics window and select another topic.

Back   To display the previously viewed Help window.

Options   To copy, print, or otherwise set preferences for
the Help window.

USING THE INDEX FEATURE

Help's Index feature provides a list of Help topics arranged alphabetically on the Index tab of the Help Topics window. Either you
can enter a word for which you are searching, or you can scroll
through the list to find a topic. Figure 5.3 shows the Index tab of
the Help Topics: Windows Help dialog box.

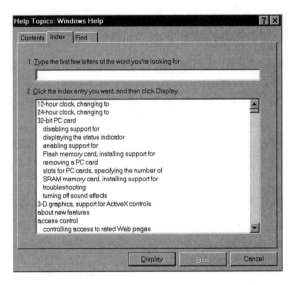

FIGURE 5.3   Use the Index tab to find specific words and phrases
in Help.

To use the Help Index, follow these steps:

1. In the Help Topics window, choose the Index tab.

2. Click the text box with the number **1** above it and type a
   topic you want to know about. As you type, Windows
   moves to the topics beginning with the first letters you
   enter.

TIP   **Browse the List**   You can scroll through the index list to see what other topics are available.

3. In the list of topics, select the topic you want to view and choose Display, or simply double-click the topic. The Help topic window appears.

4. When you're finished with the Help topic, you can choose another option, or you can close the Help window by pressing Alt+F4.

USING THE FIND FEATURE

You can search for specific words and phrases in a Help topic instead of searching for a Help topic by category. The first time you use the Find feature, however, you have to instruct Windows to create a list that contains the words from your Help files. (You only create this list once.)

The Find feature is especially useful when you cannot find a particular Help topic in Help Contents or on the Index tab's list of topics.

To use the Find feature, follow these steps:

1. In the Help Topics window, choose the Find tab. If you have used Find before, skip to the next set of steps. If you haven't set up the Help topics previously, the Find Setup Wizard dialog box appears. Continue with these steps.

2. In the Wizard dialog box, choose one of the following:

Minimize Database Size   Creates a short, limited word list (recommended because it takes less hard disk space).

Maximize Search Capabilities   Creates a long, detailed word list.

Customize Search Capabilities   Enables you to create a shorter word list, including only the Help files you want to use. Use this option if you have limited disk space. If

you select this option, choose Next, then choose the
topics you want to include.

3. Click Finish to create the word list.

When Windows finishes creating the word list, the Find tab
contains a text box, a word list, and a topic list as shown in
Figure 5.4.

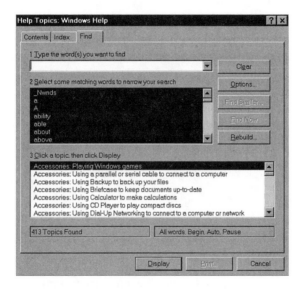

FIGURE 5.4   Windows now has a word list to search through.

To search for words or a phrase in the Find tab, follow these steps:

1. Type the word or phrase you want to find in the first text
   box at the top of the dialog box. This enters the word for
   which you want to search, and Windows displays forms
   of the word in the word list in the middle of the Find tab.

2. If you see a word that applies to your topic, select that
   word to narrow your search. If you do not want to narrow
   the search, move on to step 3.

Topic List   Instead of typing something in the text box, you can scroll through the word list and select the word you want from the list. If you want to find words similar to the words in a Help topic, click the **Find Similar** button.

3. Click one or more topics in the topic list, and then click the Display button. Windows displays the selected Help topic information in a Windows Help window.

4. When you finish with the Help topic, you can close the Help window or select another option, as described in the next section, "Using Help Windows."

Rebuild the List   If you don't want to use the first list that Windows creates, you're not stuck with it. You can rebuild the list to include more words or to exclude words. Click Rebuild and choose a word list option to recreate the word list.

USING HELP WINDOWS

When you access a Windows Help topic window, a toolbar appears at the top of the Help window and always remains visible. This toolbar includes three buttons: Help Topics, Back, and Options. Table 5.1 describes each button in the toolbar of a Windows Help window as well as the Options menu.

TABLE 5.1   WINDOWS HELP TOOLBAR BUTTONS AND MENU

BUTTON	DESCRIPTION
Help Topics	Opens the Help Topics: Windows Help window containing the Contents, Index, and Find tabs.
Back	Displays the previous Help topic window you viewed during the current session.
Options	Displays a menu containing the following commands: Annotate, Copy, Print Topic, Font, Keep Help on Top, and Use System Colors.

The following list describes the Options menu commands in more detail:

- **Annotate**   Enables you to mark any text or topic in a Help window so you can easily find the topic later. A paper clip icon appears beside any annotated text in Help.

- **Copy**   Places a copy of the text in the Help window on the Windows Clipboard for pasting to another document, application, or window.

- **Print Topic**   Sends the text in the Help window to the printer for a hard copy.

- **Font**   Select from Small, Normal, or Large type to view the help text; Normal is the default.

- **Keep Help on Top**   Choose whether to always display the Help window on top of all documents and windows so you can easily follow directions as you work.

- **Use System Colors**   Choose this option to restart the Help feature and change the colors in the Help box.

Using the What's This? Feature

The What's This? feature provides a handy way for you to get more information about dialog box options. You activate this feature by selecting the ? icon!X»at appears at the right end of the title bar in some (but not all) Windows dialog boxes. Figure 5.5 shows a window with the What's This? icon and a description you might see if you clicked on that icon.

The following steps tell you how to use the What's This? feature to display a description of most options in a Windows dialog box.

1. Click the ? icon in the upper-right corner of the Windows dialog box. A large question mark appears next to the mouse pointer.

2. Click any option in the dialog box, and Windows displays a box containing a short description of the item you selected.

3. When you finish reading the Help information, click anywhere on-screen to close the Help box.

What's This? description

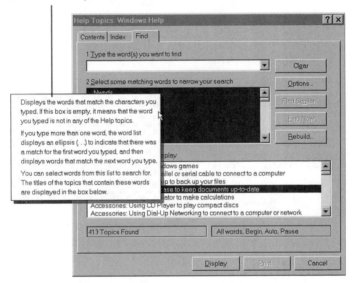

Figure 5.5 Use the What's This? feature to get help on certain dialog box elements.

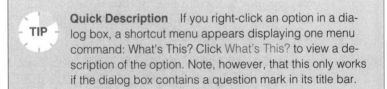

TIP

Quick Description If you right-click an option in a dialog box, a shortcut menu appears displaying one menu command: What's This? Click What's This? to view a description of the option. Note, however, that this only works if the dialog box contains a question mark in its title bar.

In this lesson, you learned how to get help, use the Help feature's shortcut buttons, and use the What's This? feature. In the next lesson, you learn to start and exit applications in Windows.

STARTING AND EXITING APPLICATIONS IN WINDOWS 95

In this lesson, you learn to start and exit a Windows 95 application as well as how to view the common elements of Windows application's screens.

OPENING A WINDOWS APPLICATION

Windows provides a Start menu from which you can perform many tasks, including starting Windows programs. To display the Start menu, click the **Start** button on the Windows taskbar. You can open the Help feature from the Start menu; you also can open various applications from the Start menu by choosing the Programs command. The menus you see stemming from the Programs menu will vary depending on your system setup (see Figure 6.1).

To open an application, follow these steps:

1. Choose the Start button.

2. Select Programs to display the Programs menu.

3. Choose the application you want to open, if it's listed on the Programs menu; alternatively, select the group containing the application you want to open.

Folder/   Right-arrow leads   Applications within   Program
Program icon   to another menu   one program group   groups

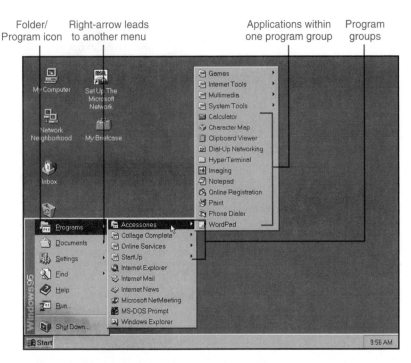

FIGURE 6.1 Access applications or other program's menus from
the Programs menu.

  TIP **Program Groups** The Programs menu displays various
group names—such as Accessories, Online Services,
StartUp, and so on—that display a menu of related applications when selected. You can identify a program group
by the Folder/Program icon in front of it and the right-
arrow following the command. Accessories, Online Services, and StartUp are installed when you install Windows.
You may also have program groups for Microsoft Office,
Lotus SmartSuite, or other applications you've installed on
your computer.

Open Documents   If you have a specific document you want to open and you've recently worked on that document, you can click the **Documents** command on the **Start** menu to display a list; click the document you want to open and the source application opens with the document, ready for you to work on.

VIEWING AN APPLICATION'S SCREEN

Depending on the application you open—whether it's a word processor, database, spreadsheet, or other program—the screen will include elements particular to the tasks and procedures used for that application. For example, the mouse may appear as an I-beam (for typing), an arrow (for pointing), or a cross (for selecting cells in a spreadsheet program); the "document" area may appear as a blank sheet of paper or a table with many cells.

Most applications, however, display the following elements: Title bar, Menu bar, Toolbars, Ruler, Scroll bars, a Document area, and a Status bar. Figure 6.2 shows the screen you see when you open the Windows accessory, WordPad.

There's Always Help   If you need help with any applications, you can click the **Help** menu in that application and select a help topic.

EXITING AN APPLICATION

You should always exit an application when you're done with it to ensure that your documents are saved before shutting Windows down. You can exit most Windows applications in one of the following ways:

- Choose the File, Exit command.
- Click the Close (X) button.
- Choose Close from the Control menu.

- Double-click the application's Control menu icon.

- Press Alt+F4.

Control menu icon   Title bar   Ruler   Menu bar   Toolbars   Minimize, Restore, and Close buttons

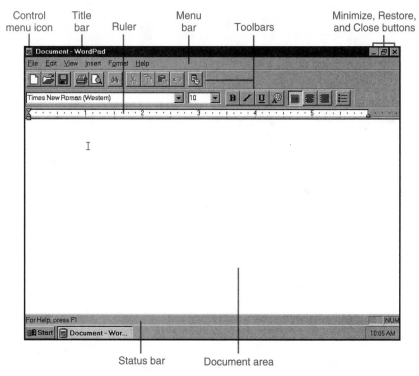

Status bar   Document area

FIGURE 6.2   Most application screens contain similar elements.

 If You Get a Message Before Closing   If the application displays a message asking you to save the document before you close the program, choose **Yes** to save, **No** to close the application without saving the changes, or **Cancel** to return to the application.

In this lesson, you learned to start and exit a Windows 95 application as well as how to view the common elements of Windows application's screens. In the next lesson, you learn to work with multiple windows.

WORKING WITH MULTIPLE WINDOWS

In this lesson, you learn how to arrange windows, switch between windows in the same application, and switch between applications.

In Windows, you can have more than one application open at a time, and in each Windows application, you can work with multiple document windows. As you can imagine, opening multiple applications with multiple windows can make your desktop pretty cluttered. That's why it's important that you know how to manipulate and switch between windows. The following sections explain how to do just that.

ARRANGING WINDOWS ON THE DESKTOP

When you have multiple windows open, some windows or parts of windows are inevitably hidden by others, which makes the screen confusing. You can use various commands to arrange your open windows. To access the cascade and tile windows commands, right-click the mouse in any open area of the taskbar and then select the command from the shortcut menu.

TIP

Quick! Clean the Desktop You can minimize all windows by choosing one command to quickly clear the desktop of open windows. Right-click the taskbar and choose Minimize All Windows. All open windows then become buttons on the taskbar.

Cascading Windows

A good way to get control of a confusing desktop is to open the
taskbar's shortcut menu and choose the **Cascade** command.
When you choose this command, Windows lays all the open windows on top of each other so that the title bar of each is visible.
Figure 7.1 shows a cascaded window arrangement using WordPad,
Solitaire, and Notepad. To access any window that's not on the
top, simply click its title bar. That window then becomes the active window.

 Active Window   The active window is the one in which
you are working. You activate a window by clicking its title
bar, or anywhere inside the window, or by clicking its button on the taskbar. The active window's title bar becomes
highlighted, and the active window comes to the front.

Other open windows   Active window

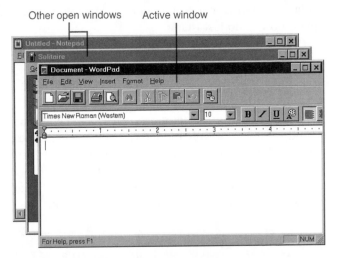

Figure 7.1   With cascaded windows, you can easily access the
one you need.

You can still click and drag the title bar of any window to another location on the desktop and you can use the mouse to resize the window borders of any open window, even when it is cascaded with other windows.

TILING WINDOWS

If you need to see all open windows at the same time, open the taskbar's shortcut menu and select either the **Tile Horizontally** or the **Tile Vertically** command. When you choose to tile, Windows resizes and moves each open window so that they all appear side-by-side (vertically) or one on top of the other (horizontally), as shown in Figure 7.2.

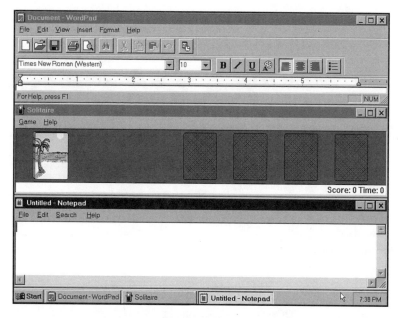

FIGURE 7.2   Tile windows so you can see a part of each window at the same time.

MOVING BETWEEN APPLICATIONS

Windows enables you to have multiple applications open at the same time. If the open application windows are not maximized, you might be able to see all of those open windows overlapped on-screen. In this case, you can click any window to bring it forward. Often, however, it's easier to work in a single application by maximizing the application's window. Switching between applications then requires a different procedure. You'll most likely use the taskbar to switch from application to application by clicking the minimized application button on the taskbar.

After opening several applications—such as WordPad, Paint, and Solitaire, for example—you can use the taskbar by following these steps:

> **1.** On the taskbar, click the button representing the application you want to bring forward (see Figure 7.3).

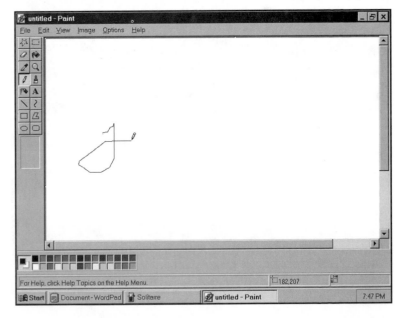

FIGURE 7.3 All open and minimized application windows appear on the taskbar.

2. To switch to another open application, click its button on the taskbar. The open window minimizes back to the taskbar and is replaced by the next application you select.

MOVING BETWEEN WINDOWS IN THE SAME APPLICATION

In addition to working in multiple applications in Windows, you also can open multiple windows within an application. Moving to a new window means you are changing the window that is active. If you are using a mouse, you can move to a window by clicking any part of it. When you do, the title bar becomes highlighted, and that particular window comes to the front so you can work in it.

Figure 7.4 shows multiple document windows open in Microsoft Word. You can switch between the windows, arrange windows, and open and close windows within the application, just as you can manipulate windows within the Windows 95 program.

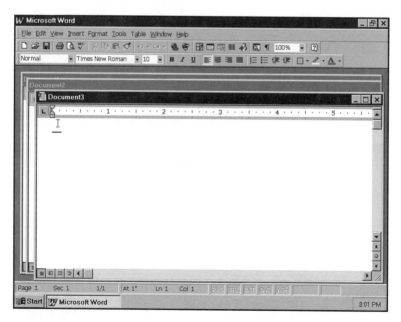

FIGURE 7.4   Three document windows are open within the program.

Open multiple document windows using the File, Open command. By default, each window is maximized within the document area. To switch between open, maximized windows, click the Window menu and select the document from the list at the bottom of the menu. Alternatively, you can press **Ctrl+F6** to cycle through open windows.

To view multiple document windows on-screen, follow these steps:

1. Restore the document window by clicking the document's Restore button. The open document windows cascade in the document area. The Restore button replaces the Maximize button.

2. To activate an open document window, click in the window's title bar or press Ctrl+F6.

3. To tile the windows, choose Window, Arrange All. Windows reduces each open document window and tiles them (horizontally) in the document area.

 TIP **They're All Just Windows**   You can use the window frames to resize each window. Likewise, you can minimize, maximize, open, and close the windows as you would any window. (See Lesson 2 for instructions.)

In this lesson, you learned how to arrange windows, switch between windows in the same application, and switch between applications. In the next lesson, you learn to copy and move information between windows.

COPYING AND MOVING INFORMATION BETWEEN WINDOWS

In this lesson, you learn about the Clipboard and how to copy and move information between windows.

WHAT IS THE CLIPBOARD?

One of the handiest features of the Windows environment is its capability to copy or move information (text, graphics, and files) from one location to another. This feature enables you to share information between document windows, applications, and other computers on your network.

When you cut or copy data from an application, it's placed on the Clipboard and it remains there until you cut or copy again. You can paste the data from the Clipboard to a document or application. Note, however, that you don't have to open the Clipboard to use it—and 99 percent of the time, you won't. You'll just cut or copy your data, and then paste it to a new location.

Copy, Cut, and Paste When you copy information, the application copies it to the Clipboard without disturbing the original. When you cut information, the application removes it from its original location and places it on the Clipboard. When you paste information, the application inserts the information that's on the Clipboard in the location you specify. (The copy on the Clipboard remains intact, so you can paste it again and again, if necessary.)

You can view the information on the Clipboard viewer, if you want, by choosing Start, Programs, Accessories, and Clipboard Viewer (see Figure 8.1). In the Viewer, you can save the contents to a file name, add or remove text, edit the text, and open saved Clipboard files.

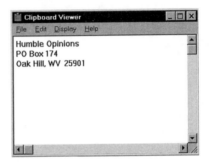

FIGURE 8.1   View and even save the contents of the Clipboard, if you want.

    Without a Trace   When you turn off your computer or exit Windows, the contents of the Clipboard disappear. Be sure you save the contents of the Clipboard if you want to use the text or figures later.

SELECTING TEXT FOR COPYING OR MOVING

Before you can copy or cut text, you must identify the text by selecting it. Selected text appears in reverse video (highlighted). Figure 8.2 shows selected text in a WordPad document.

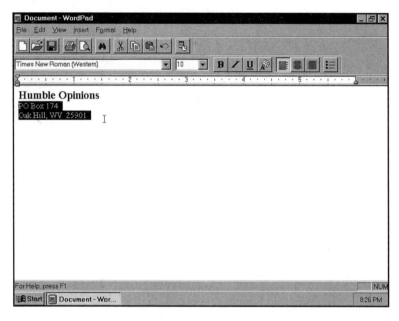

FIGURE 8.2   You must first select text before you can cut or copy it.

To select text, follow these steps:

1. Position the mouse pointer just before the first character you want to select.

2. Press and hold the left mouse button, and drag the mouse pointer to the last character you want selected.

3. Release the mouse button, and the selected text is high-lighted.

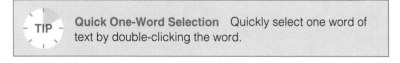

TIP   **Quick One-Word Selection**   Quickly select one word of text by double-clicking the word.

Where's My Selected Text? If you press an alphanumeric key (a letter, number, or any other character) while text is highlighted, Windows deletes the selected text and replaces it with the character you typed. Choose **Edit**, **Undo** or press **Ctrl+Z** (in most applications) to reverse the action.

SELECTING GRAPHICS

The procedure for selecting graphics depends on the Windows application you are using. In a word processing program, such as WordPad or Microsoft Word, you select a graphic by clicking the object. In a program like Paint, however, there are special tools for selecting shapes. Because the procedure may vary, you should refer to the instructions for each application. No matter how you select a graphic, however, when it's selected, small "handles" appear on the corners and sides of the graphic frame to indicate it is ready to be copied or moved.

COPYING INFORMATION BETWEEN WINDOWS

After you select text or graphics, the procedures for copying and pasting are the same in all Windows applications. To copy and paste information between windows of the same application, as well as between windows of different applications, follow these steps:

1. Select the text or graphic to copy.

2. Click the Copy button on the toolbar, or choose Edit, Copy. You can, alternatively, use a keyboard shortcut, such as **Ctrl+C** for copy. A copy of the selected material is placed on the Clipboard; the original selection remains in place.

3. Click to position the insertion point where you want to insert the selection. You can switch between document windows or between applications as learned in Lesson 7.

4. Click the Paste button, choose Edit, Paste, or press **Ctrl+V**. Windows copies the selection from the Clipboard to the insertion point.

 TIP   **Multiple Copies**   Because the selected item remains on the Clipboard until you copy or cut again, you can paste information from the Clipboard multiple times.

MOVING INFORMATION BETWEEN WINDOWS

After you select text or graphics, the procedures for cutting and pasting are also the same in all Windows applications. To cut and paste information between windows of the same application or windows of different applications, follow these steps:

1. Select the text or graphic.

2. Click the Cut button, choose Edit, Cut, or press **Ctrl+X.** Windows removes the selection from its original location and places it on the Clipboard.

3. Click to position the insertion point to where you want to insert the selection.

4. Click the Paste button, choose Edit, Paste, or press **Ctrl+V**. Windows copies the selection from the Clipboard to your document. (A copy remains on the Clipboard until you cut or copy something else.)

In this lesson, you learned about the Clipboard and how to copy and move information between windows. In the next lesson, you learn to view drives, folders, and files in the Windows Explorer.

9 VIEWING DRIVES, FOLDERS, AND FILES WITH THE WINDOWS EXPLORER

In this lesson, you learn how to use the Windows Explorer to view contents of a hard disk drive, floppy disk, or CD-ROM.

STARTING THE WINDOWS EXPLORER

You use the Explorer to organize, rename, copy, move, delete, and otherwise manage your folders (directories) and files. Start the Explorer from the Start menu. Click the Start button and choose Programs, Windows Explorer. The Windows Explorer window opens.

USING THE EXPLORER WINDOW

At the top of the Explorer window, Windows gives the name of the drive whose contents you are currently viewing. In addition, the Explorer window is split into two panes. By default, the left pane displays your hard disk and the folders it contains. The right pane displays a list of the files stored in the selected folder. Figure 9.1 shows the Explorer window.

Table 9.1 describes the elements in the Explorer window. If you do not see a toolbar or status bar on your screen, open the View menu and select the item you want to display.

FIGURE 9.1   Use the Explorer to manage your drives.

TABLE 9.1 EXPLORER WINDOW ELEMENTS

ELEMENT	DESCRIPTION
Title bar	Contains the window name (Exploring), the drive name, a Control menu, and the Minimize, Maximize, and Close buttons for the Explorer.
Menu bar	Displays menus related to disk, folder, file, and other operations.
Drive window path	Displays the current drive, and/or path, in the toolbar.

continues

TABLE 9.1   CONTINUED

ELEMENT	DESCRIPTION
Drive and folder pane	Displays drives, folders, and subfolders as well as the recycle bin and the brief-case.
Folder, file, and subfolder pane	Displays the contents of the selected drive or folder in the left pane.
Toolbar	Provides various tools for navigating the Explorer.
Status bar	Displays such statistics as free space on drive, number of files in a folder, and so on.

Subfolders   A subfolder is a folder within another folder—the same thing as a subdirectory.

TIP   **Folder and File Icons**   Each folder has a folder icon beside it, and each file has an icon that represents its file type (such as a sheet of paper for a document, window box for an executable program, and so on).

The Explorer also offers several tool buttons you can use to speed your work. Tool buttons represent common menu commands. Table 9.2 shows the tool buttons on the Explorer's toolbar and explains their functions.

TABLE 9.2   TOOLBAR BUTTONS

TOOL	NAME	DESCRIPTION
(C:) ▾	Go to a Different Folder	Click to view a drop-down box of available drives and folders

TOOL	NAME	DESCRIPTION
	Up One Level	Click to go to the parent folder of the current folder; for example, if you're in the My Documents folder, clicking this icon takes you to drive C
	Map Network Drive	Use this tool to create a mapped drive to a network drive for quick access of a server's resources
	Disconnect Net Drive	Click to disconnect from the network
	Cut	Cut the selected file or folder to the Clipboard
	Copy	Copy the selected file or folder to the Clipboard
	Paste	Paste the contents on the Clipboard to the current location
	Undo	Reverse the last action you performed; some actions cannot be undone
	Delete	Erases the selected file or folder
	Properties	Displays the properties of the selected file or folder, including rights, name, size, date created, and so on
	Large Icons	Click to change the view of your files and folders to large icons with the names of the file or folder below the icon

continues

TABLE 9.2 CONTINUED

Tool	Name	Description
	Small Icons	Click to change the view to small icons with the name of the file or folder
	List	Click to change the view to a list of the names of the files and folders
	Details	Click to change the view to a list of the file or folder name, the creation or modification date, size, and file type

To display drives, folders, and files, follow these steps:

1. In the left pane, scroll the list of drives and folders using the scroll bar. The list displays floppy drives, hard drives, CD drives, the Network Neighborhood, and so on. Select the drive you want to view by clicking it.

2. In the left pane, double-click any folder to display its additional folders in the folder pane.

3. In the right pane, click a folder once to display its contents (files and folders).

VIEWING FOLDERS

Collapsed folders are represented by a plus sign (+) in the folders pane of the Explorer window; expanded folders are represented by a minus sign (–). Figure 9.2 shows both collapsed and expanded folders.

To expand a folder so you can view its contents, click the plus sign preceding the folder in the folders pane of the Explorer window. To collapse a folder to hide its contents, click the minus sign preceding the folder.

Collapsed folders

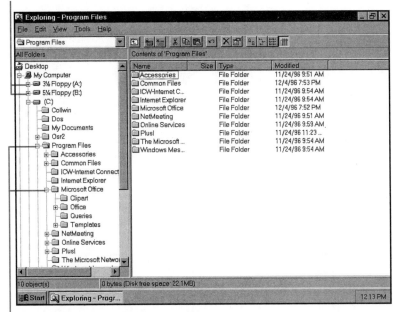

Expanded folders

FIGURE 9.2 Expand a folder to see its contents; collapse it to hide its contents.

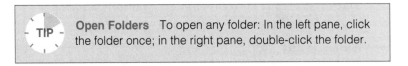

Open Folders To open any folder: In the left pane, click the folder once; in the right pane, double-click the folder.

VIEWING AND SORTING FILES

In addition to the file name, you can view various details about the files in a folder: the date created, file type, and file size.

To view file details, simply choose View, Details. Windows displays the file name, type, size, and creation or modification date (see Figure 9.3).

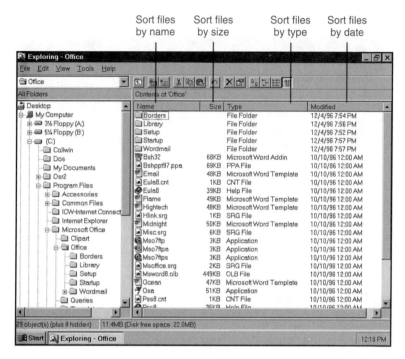

FIGURE 9.3   You might need to see the file details to determine files you want to copy, delete, or otherwise manipulate.

You also can use the heading buttons in the files pane to sort the files. To sort files, click one of the heading buttons shown in Figure 9.3 and described here:

Sort files by name   Alphabetically sorts files by name, A to Z on the first click and Z to A on the second click.

Sort files by type   Alphabetically sorts files by the file type (application, font, help, document, and so on), A to Z on the first click and Z to A on the second click. Notice folders come first in the A to Z sort.

Sort files by size   Sorts files by size, largest to smallest on the first click and smallest to largest on the second click.

Sort files by date   Sorts files by date, earliest files created first on the first click and most recently created or modified files first on the second click.

 Another Sort Method   You can choose the **View menu**, **Arrange Icons** command and choose to sort the files by **Name**, **Type**, **Size**, or **Date** using the secondary menu.

CLOSING THE EXPLORER

To close the Windows Explorer, choose File, Close, or click the Close button.

In this lesson, you learned how to use the Windows Explorer to view a disk's contents. In the next lesson, you learn to create and delete files and folders.

10

CREATING AND DELETING FILES AND FOLDERS

In this lesson, you learn how to create folders, how to delete files and folders, and how to use the Recycle Bin.

CREATING A FOLDER

Many folders are created automatically when you install a program. For example, when you install Word for Windows, the installation program creates a folder on your hard disk and places the Word for Windows files in that folder. You can use an application's designated document folder, or you can create folders yourself. For example, you might create a folder to hold any of the following groups of files:

- Subject-related files (such as all sales documents, whether they are word processing, accounting, or spreadsheet files, for example).

- Application-related files (such as all word processing files or, more specifically, all letters to customers).

- The files for an application that does not create its own folder during installation.

- All files you'll share with other network users.

To create a folder using the Explorer, follow these steps:

1. From the Desktop, choose Start, Programs, and Windows Explorer. The Explorer window opens.

2. In the Drive Window Path on the toolbar, click the drop-down arrow. From the drop-down list, select the drive on which you want to create the new folder.

3. In the left pane, select the folder in which you want the new folder located. This is often called the parent or root folder of your new folder.

Root, Parent Folders The root folder is the same as the drive. For example, C is the root folder of the hard disk. The root folder is also the parent of all folders on that drive, and a folder is the parent to all folders it contains.

4. Choose File, New, Folder, and a new folder appears in the right pane, with the name "New Folder."

5. Type a name for the new folder in the highlighted text box (see Figure 10.1).

6. Press Enter to complete the process.

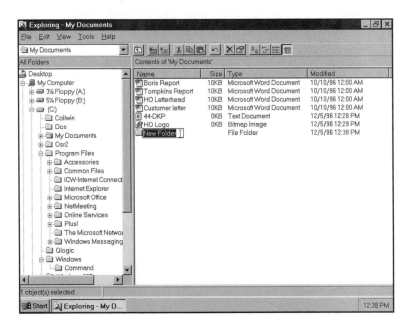

FIGURE 10.1 Add a folder to help organize your work.

TIP   **Rename a Folder** To rename a folder, select the folder in the Explorer and choose File, Rename. The folder's name appears highlighted in a box; type the new name and press Enter to finish. You can, alternatively, click the folder name after selecting it to display the mouse I-beam, the highlighted word, and the box used for renaming; however, be careful not to double-click the folder's name or you'll open the folder instead of renaming it.

DELETING A FILE OR FOLDER

You should delete a file or folder when you no longer need it, when your disk is getting full, or when you created the file or folder by mistake. Before you delete anything, however, it is a good idea to make a backup copy in case you discover a need for it later; copy to a floppy disk if you're trying to save disk space. See Lesson 11 for directions on how to copy files and folders.

In Windows, deleted items are moved to an area called the Recycle Bin and remain there until you empty the bin. Deleting items to the Recycle Bin does not provide any extra disk space. Those items remain on the disk until you empty the Recycle Bin. We'll talk more about the Recycle Bin later in this lesson.

To delete a file or folder, follow these steps:

1. In the Explorer, select the file or folder you want to delete by clicking it. You can select multiple files or folders by holding the Ctrl key as you click the file you want to select.

TIP   **Selecting More Than One** For more about selecting files and folders, see Lesson 11.

Oops, Wrong Folder   If you delete a parent folder, Windows also deletes everything in that folder. Be careful to delete only those files and folders you no longer need.

2. Choose File, Delete or press the Delete key. The Delete dialog box appears, asking you to confirm that you want to delete the specified item(s) (see Figure 10.2).

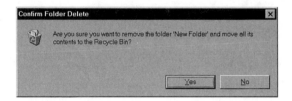

FIGURE 10.2   Delete unwanted files and/or folders.

3. Select Yes and Windows moves the item to the Recycle Bin.

USING THE RECYCLE BIN

The Windows Recycle Bin holds deleted files and folders until you empty the bin or recover the files. You can open the Recycle Bin at any time to view the items in it.

EMPTYING THE BIN

You can empty the Recycle Bin from Explorer or from the Desktop. You should check the Bin's contents before you empty it to be sure you're not deleting something you really want. You can view the Bin from the Explorer or from the Desktop.

To view and then empty the Recycle Bin, follow these steps:

1. In the Explorer, scroll to the bottom of the left pane until you see the Recycle Bin.

2. Click the Recycle Bin to display its contents in the right pane (see Figure 10.3).

Recycle Bin   Deleted files

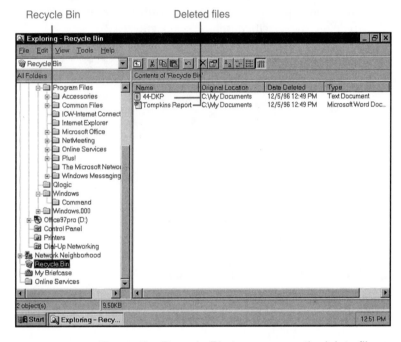

FIGURE 10.3   Empty the Recycle Bin to permanently delete files from you hard drive.

3. To empty the Bin, choose R. Windows displays a Confirmation dialog box.

4. Choose Yes to delete the files.

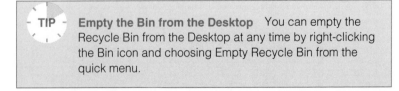

- TIP -   **Empty the Bin from the Desktop**   You can empty the Recycle Bin from the Desktop at any time by right-clicking the Bin icon and choosing Empty Recycle Bin from the quick menu.

Permanently Deleted Files   Once you empty the Recycle Bin, those files and folders are deleted and cannot be retrieved.

RECOVERING DELETED FILES FROM THE BIN

You can move files and folders to the Recycle Bin and then change your mind before deleting them completely from disk. When you recover a file or folder from the Bin, you're simply moving it back to its original drive and folder.

To recover files in the Recycle Bin, follow these steps:

1. In the Explorer, open the Recycle Bin so you can view the files and folders it contains.

2. Select any files or folders you want to recover and choose File, Restore. Windows moves the selected files and folders back to their original place on your hard drive.

In this lesson, you learned how to create folders, how to delete files and folders, and how to use the Recycle Bin. In the next lesson, you learn to move, copy, and rename files and folders.

11

SELECTING, MOVING, AND COPYING FILES AND FOLDERS

In this lesson, you learn how to select multiple files and folders and how to copy and move them.

SELECTING MULTIPLE FILES OR FOLDERS

To speed up operations, you can select multiple files or folders and then perform an action—such as copying, moving, deleting, or printing—on the entire group. For example, you may want to select several files to copy to a disk. Copying them all at once is much faster than copying each file individually. You select multiple files and folders in one of two ways, depending on whether they are contiguous or noncontiguous in the Explorer window.

 Contiguous When the files that you want to select are listed next to each other in the Explorer without any files that you don't want in between them, they are contiguous.

SELECTING MULTIPLE CONTIGUOUS FILES OR FOLDERS

To select contiguous files or folders with the mouse, follow these steps:

1. In the Explorer, click the first file or folder you want to select, and it becomes highlighted.

It's Not Working! You cannot select multiple folders in the left pane; you can only select multiple folders listed in the right pane.

2. Hold down the Shift key and click the last file or folder that you want to select. Windows highlights all the items between (and including) the first and last selections. Figure 11.1 shows a selection of contiguous files.

3. To deselect all selected items with the mouse, click any one file or folder. To deselect only one or two items, continue to hold the Shift key, and then click the selected items you want to deselect.

Selected files   Selected folders

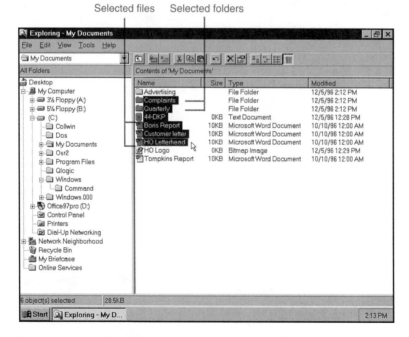

FIGURE 11.1 Select two or more contiguous files or folders by holding the Shift key as you click the files with the mouse.

SELECTING NONCONTIGUOUS FILES OF FOLDERS

Often, the files or folders you want to select are noncontiguous—separated by several files you do not want to select. To select non-contiguous files or folders, use the Ctrl key.

To select noncontiguous files or folders, follow these steps:

1. Select the first file or folder.

2. Hold down the Ctrl key and click the subsequent files or folders you want to select. Each item you select becomes highlighted and remains highlighted unless and until you deselect the items. Release the Ctrl key when you've completed your selection. Figure 11.2 shows a selections of multiple noncontiguous files and folders.

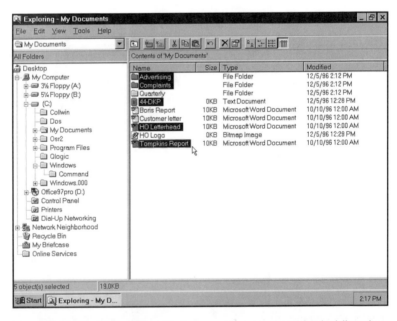

FIGURE 11.2 Select files that are not in sequence by holding the Ctrl key when you click.

3. To deselect all selected items with the mouse, click any one folder or file. To deselect only one or two items,

continue to hold the Ctrl key, then click the selected items to deselect them.

 TIP **Selecting All Files** If you want to select all of the files in the right pane of the Explorer, press Ctrl+A or choose Edit, Select All.

MOVING OR COPYING FILES OR FOLDERS

The time will come when you will want to rearrange files and folders on your system. For example, you might need to move a file from a folder of word processing files to a folder of files related to a particular subject. Or, you might want to copy files you've created into a folder to which certain other users have access. Windows provides you with two methods for doing this: menu commands and drag-and-drop.

Before you begin moving or copying files, take these warnings into consideration:

- When you copy or move a folder, you also copy or move the files and other folders within the folder.

- If you move application files to another folder, you may have trouble starting the application through the Start, Programs menu. Your best bet is to leave application files in their original locations.

USING DRAG-AND-DROP

The easiest way to move or copy files and folders to a new location in the Explorer is to use drag-and-drop. To drag-and-drop, you select the items you want from your source folder, hold down the mouse button, drag the mouse to the destination folder, and release the mouse button.

Specifically, follow these steps to use the drag-and-drop method of copying or moving files:

1. In the right pane, display the folder or file you want to move or copy.

2. Select the files you want to copy or move.

3. To copy the files, point to any one of the selected files, press and hold the Ctrl key, press the mouse button, and drag the files to the folder or drive icon where you want the copy placed.

   To move the files, point to any of the selected files, press the mouse button, and then drag the files to the folder or drive icon to which you want to move the files.

 Confirm File Replace   If you attempt to copy or move a file or folder to a location in which a file or folder with the same name exists, Windows lets you know with a message that displays the selected file's and the original file's size and creation or modification date. Click **Yes** to replace the file, or **No** to stop the process.

Using the Menus

You can use the Copy and Cut commands on the Edit menu to move or copy files and folders. To use the menus to copy or move selected files or folders, follow these steps:

1. Select the files and/or folders you want to move or copy.

2. Open the Edit menu and select Cut or Copy. The selected items are either moved or copied to the Clipboard.

 Quick Cut, Copy, Paste   As an alternative to using the Edit menu to cut, copy, and/or paste, you can click the Cut, Copy, or Paste tool button on the Explorer toolbar to accomplish the same task.

3. In the left pane of the explorer, select the drive or folder in which you want to move or copy the selected files and/or folders.

4. Choose the Edit menu and the Paste command. Windows moves or copies the selected files or folders to the new location.

In this lesson, you learned how to select multiple files and folders and how to copy and move them. In the next lesson, you learn to find files and folders in Windows 95.

12

RENAMING AND FINDING FILES AND FOLDERS

In this lesson, you learn how to rename files and folders and how to find files and folders.

RENAMING FILES OR FOLDERS

You might rename a file or folder to reorganize or update your work; you might rename files to convert from the old eight-character names to longer, more descriptive ones. The more files and folders you create and use, the more likely it is that you will need to rename them at some point.

To rename a file or folder, follow these steps:

1. In the Explorer, select the file or folder you want to rename.

2. Choose File, Rename. The current name becomes highlighted and appears in a box with the mouse I-beam, as shown in Figure 12.1.

3. Enter the new name for the file or folder.

4. Press Enter. The new name appears beside the file or folder's icon.

But It Worked Yesterday!   Never rename program files (most have extensions EXE, COM, PIF, or BAT). Many applications will not work if their files have been renamed. Also, don't rename any files with the INI or DLL extensions; these are configuration files that Windows needs to properly operate.

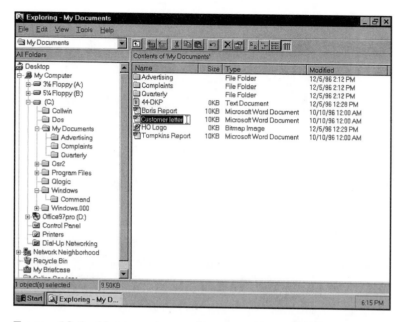

FIGURE 12.1   You can change the name of a file or folder quickly and easily.

SEARCHING FOR A FILE

The Windows Find program (**Start** menu, **Find**, **Files and Folders**) works similarly to the Explorer's Find program. You can find a specific file, files with specific extensions, files for which you have a partial name, and more.

To search for a file, follow these steps:

1. From the Windows Explorer, choose Tools, Find, Files and Folders. The find dialog box appears with the Name & Location tab open (see Figure 12.2).

2. In the **Named** text box, type the name of the file or folder you want to find (use wild cards in place of unknown characters, if you want).

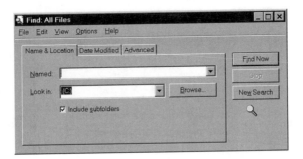

FIGURE 12.2   Tell Windows what to search for and where to begin the search

Wild Card   A character that fills in for other character(s) in a file name. When you're not sure of the file name you want to find or you're searching for more than one file with a similar extension of naming pattern, you can use the asterisk wild card (*) to replace multiple characters in the actual name, such as *.DOC (find all documents ending with the DOC extension). You can also use the question mark wild card (?) to replace one character in the file name, such as proj04??.doc. This search pattern will find files named proj04aa.doc, proj04ab.doc, or even proj0431.doc, for example.

3. In the **Look In** text box, enter the drive and/or folders you want to search. If you enter **C:**, for example, Windows searches all of drive C. You can, alternatively, choose the **Browse** button to select the drive or folder you want to search.

Browse?   When you click the Browse button, a dialog box appears in which you can choose the drive and folder you want to use. Double-click any drive or folder to open it and view its contents. Select the drive and folder you want to search and close the dialog box. The selected drive and folder appear in the Look In text box.

4. Click the Include subfolders option to put a checkmark in it. This tells Windows to search all subfolders within the folders you've specified for the search.

5. Choose Find Now, and Windows searches for the files that meet your criteria. When it finishes the search, you see the results at the bottom of the Find dialog box. Figure 12.3 shows the results of the search C:*.doc. Notice that the title bar of the Find dialog box includes search criteria.

6. When you finish checking out the results, close the Find dialog box.

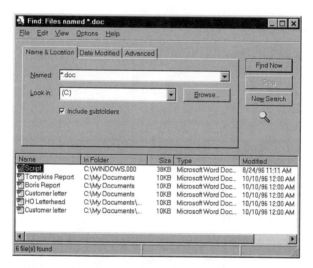

FIGURE 12.3 The results of the search for DOC files.

In this lesson, you learned how to rename files and folders and how to find files and folders. In the next lesson, you learn to create a document with WordPad.

LESSON 13

CREATING A DOCUMENT WITH WORDPAD

In this lesson, you learn how to create, edit, format, and save a document in WordPad.

CREATING AND EDITING A DOCUMENT

You can use Window's word processing program called WordPad to create a document such as a letter, memo, report, list, or newsletter. Although WordPad is a word processor, it is a very basic application. For example, you cannot check your spelling or grammar in WordPad, and there are only a limited number of toolbars and icons to help speed your work. However, you can create, edit, and format many simple documents with WordPad. Basically, it's fine to use if you don't have another word processor such as Word or Word Pro.

To create a document in Word Pad, follow these steps:

1. From the Desktop, choose the Start button, and select Programs, then Accessories.

2. Click the WordPad option at the bottom of the Accessories menu. The program appears with a new, untitled document in the window for you to use, as shown in Figure 13.1.

A blinking vertical bar, called the insertion point, appears in the upper-left corner of the document area.

 Insertion Point The point at which the text you type will appear.

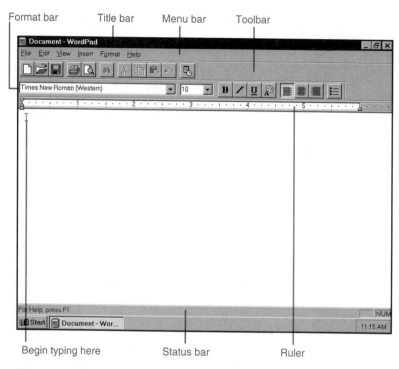

Format bar   Title bar   Menu bar   Toolbar

Begin typing here   Status bar   Ruler

FIGURE 13.1   Use the WordPad program to create documents.

Like most word processing programs, WordPad has text-wrapping; you needn't press Enter at the end of each line. Press Enter only to mark the end of a paragraph or to insert a blank line on the page.

The WordPad screen contains the following elements:

- The application name (WordPad) and the document name (the generic name is Document until you assign a name by saving the document) in the title bar.

- The menu bar containing WordPad menus.

- Two toolbars containing shortcuts for saving and formatting your documents.

- A ruler that enables you to set tabs and measure margins.

- The text insertion point, which marks the location of the text you enter.

- A status bar that offers helpful tips and information about the program.

Windows Elements Note that the WordPad window contains many elements other windows do: Minimize, Maximize, and Close buttons, a Control Menu button, a window border if the window is restored, and so on. For more information, see Lesson 2.

Need Help? The Help feature in WordPad works similarly to the Help feature in any window or program. So if you need help, access the Help menu.

MOVING THE TEXT INSERTION POINT

To move the insertion point with the mouse, just click the place in the text to which you want to move to. To move the insertion point using the keyboard, see the options in Table 13.1. You can use these keys to move the insertion point around without disturbing existing text. You cannot move the insertion point beyond the last character in your document.

TABLE 13.1 **MOVING THE INSERTION POINT WITH THE KEYBOARD**

PRESS	TO MOVE
Down arrow	Down one line
Up arrow	Up one line
Right arrow	Right one character
Left arrow	Left one character

PRESS	TO MOVE
Page Up	Previous screen
Page Down	Next screen
Ctrl+Right arrow	Next word
Ctrl+Left arrow	Previous word
Ctrl+PageUp	Top of screen
Ctrl+PageDown	Bottom of screen
Home	Beginning of line
End	End of line
Ctrl+Home	Beginning of document
Ctrl+End	End of document

INSERTING AND DELETING TEXT

To insert text within existing text, simply place the insertion point in the appropriate location (using the mouse or the keyboard) and begin typing. The existing characters move to the right as you type to make room for the new text.

To delete a single character to the left of the insertion point, press the Backspace key. To delete the character to the right of the insertion point, press the Delete key. To delete larger amounts of text, select the text and press the Delete key (see the next section to find out how to select text).

SELECTING, CUTTING, COPYING, AND PASTING TEXT

Before you can work with text, you must select it. To select text with the mouse, click at the beginning of the text and drag the I-beam pointer over the text so that it appears highlighted. To select text with the keyboard, place the insertion point at the beginning of the text, press and hold the Shift key, and use the techniques described in Table 13.1 to move to the end of the text you want to select. When you release the Shift key, the text you marked appears highlighted.

WordPad uses the Windows Clipboard to store cut and copied text until you cut or copy again. To cut and copy text, select the text first and then use the Edit menu or the Cut and Copy buttons on the toolbar. Cut or copy, move the insertion point to the location in which you want to paste the text and then choose Edit, Paste or the button on the toolbar.

FORMATTING A DOCUMENT

You can affect the appearance of your document on-screen and on-paper by changing the formatting. Formatting refers to the appearance of a document, including the font style and size, text alignment, and page layout.

You can format text before or after you type it. To format text before you type it, choose the formatting attributes and then enter the text; the formatting continues until you change the formatting again. To format text after you type it, select the text you want to change and then apply the specific formatting changes.

CHANGING FONT, FONT STYLE, AND FONT SIZE

You can change the following text attributes to improve the appearance of your text or to set it apart from other text:

Font   Choose from Arial, Times New Roman, and so on to change the look of the text.

Font Style   Apply Bold, Italic, Bold Italic, Underline, Superscript, or Subscript attributes to change the style of the text.

Font Size   Choose from 10-point, 12-point, 72-point and everything in between and even larger to change the size of your type for headlines, fine print, and so on. (There are about 72 points in an inch.)

To change the font, font style, or font size, follow these steps:

1. Select the text to be formatted.

2. Choose Format, Font from the WordPad menu bar. The Font dialog box appears (see Figure 13.2).

Change the font here   Change the style attributes here   Change the font size here

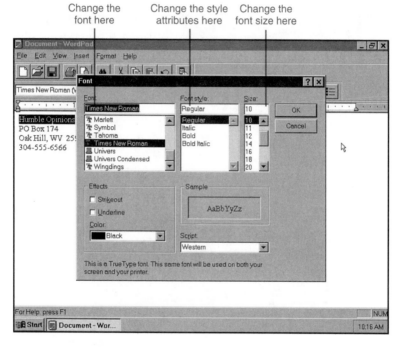

FIGURE 13.2   Change the look of the text on the page in WordPad.

3. Select the font, font style, and size options you want. The Sample Area shows sample text with options you selected.

4. Choose OK to apply the changes.

TIP   **Quickie Formatting**   Use the Format bar above the ruler to select a font, size, or attribute to apply to selected text. Just click the down arrow beside the font or size drop-down list; or click the Bold, Italic, or Underline buttons on the Formatting tool bar to apply a style attribute.

Figure 13.3 shows a document with formatting applied to selected text. Note that you can use multiple fonts and font sizes to add interest and emphasis.

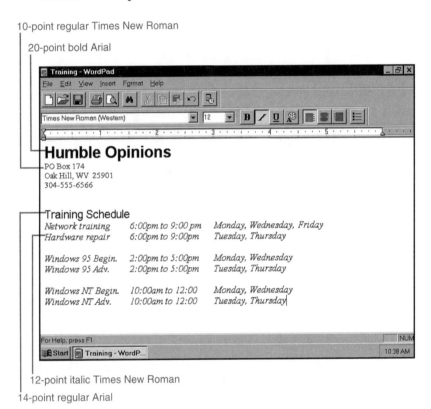

FIGURE 13.3 You can vary the font, size, and style of text within your document to add emphasis to important text.

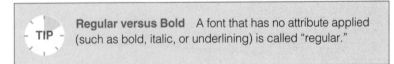

Regular versus Bold A font that has no attribute applied (such as bold, italic, or underlining) is called "regular."

MODIFYING TEXT ALIGNMENT

Normally, text is aligned with the left margin. However, you can right-align text or center it between the margins.

Alignment Left-aligned text is flush along the left edge of the page and ragged along the right edge; left-aligned text is the default alignment for most word processing programs. Right-aligned text is the opposite of left-aligned. Centered text is ragged on both the left and right sides, but each line is centered between the two side margins. Justified text makes the text flush with both the left and right edges of the page; however, WordPad doesn't support justified text.

To align text, follow these steps:

1. Select the text.

2. Use the formatting toolbar buttons to choose the alignment:

    Left

    Center

    Right

ADJUSTING PAGE MARGINS

You can change the page margins using the Page Setup dialog box. You also can choose page size and orientation in this same dialog box.

Page Settings Before you change your paper size, source, or orientation of the page, check your printer documentation to verify it can print to a special setting. Many printers, for example, cannot print to small note paper or A4 envelopes and most printers have a required margin (usually at least .25 inch).

To change page margins, follow these steps:

1. Choose File, Page Setup. The Page Setup dialog box appears, as shown in Figure 13.4.

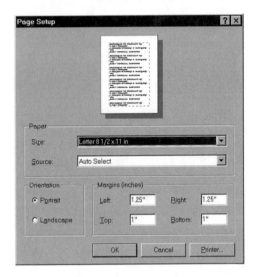

FIGURE 13.4 Change the margins in the Page Setup dialog box.

2. In the Margins area, enter new measurements in the Left, Right, Top, or Bottom text boxes. The default measurement is inches.

3. Choose OK to apply the margins to your document.

Paper Size Changes Click the drop-down arrow beside Size in the Paper area to select another size paper, such as #10 commercial size envelope or 8¹/₂-by-14-inch paper. You also can choose the paper tray or envelope feeder, if applicable, from the Source drop-down list.

SAVING A DOCUMENT AND EXITING WORDPAD

To avoid losing the changes you've made to your WordPad document file, you need to save your work often. The first time you save a document, you assign it a name and location on the disk. After the first time, you can simply save changes to the same named document. If you attempt to exit WordPad or close the file, WordPad will ask if you want to save the document.

To save a WordPad document, follow these steps:

1. Choose File, Save As. The Save As dialog box (shown in Figure 13.5) appears.

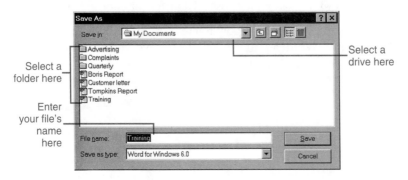

FIGURE 13.5 Give the file a name and choose a location on the disk.

Save As or Save?   Choose Save As to assign a file name and a location to your document the first time you save it or any time you want to save a file under a new name or location. Choose Save to save any changes you make to a document that's already been named.

2. In the Save In drop-down list, choose a drive to save the file to.

3. In the list box, double-click the folder in which you want to save the file.

4. In the **File Name** text box, enter a name for the file; you can take advantage of Windows long file names by entering letters, numbers, and using spaces that exceed the previous DOS eight-letter limitations.

5. Choose Save. Windows saves the file, closes the dialog box, and returns to the document on-screen. The name in the title bar changes from "Untitled" to the name you assigned your document.

To exit WordPad, click the Close (X) button or choose File, Exit.

In this lesson, you learned how to create, edit, format, and save a document in WordPad. In the next lesson, you learn to use the Windows accessory, Paint.

ADDING GRAPHICS WITH PAINT

In this lesson, you learn to open the Paint program, create a drawing with Paint, and save the drawing.

OPENING PAINT

Paint allows you to give all of your documents—invoices, letters, reports, and so on—an artistic touch. You can produce simple or complicated drawings to add to your documents, and you can use your creations in other Windows applications such as Word or Word Pro.

To open the Paint program and begin a drawing, follow these steps:

1. From the Desktop, choose the Start button and then Programs, Accessories.

2. Click Paint from the Accessories menu. The Paint window shown in Figure 14.1 appears, ready for you to draw.

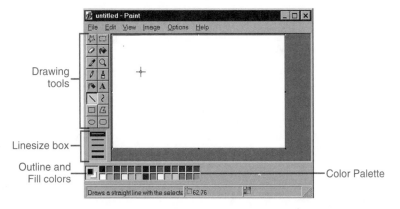

FIGURE 14.1 Use the Paint tools and menus to create a drawing.

In addition to the standard application window parts, the Paint window shown in the figure also has a set of drawing tools (called the toolbox) on the left and a color palette at the bottom of the window.

Outline and Fill Colors   The overlapping boxes to the left of the color palette show the currently selected outline color (the box on top and to the left) and the fill color (the box underneath and to the right). The outline color is the color you'll use when you draw lines and outlines for objects, and the fill color is the color of the inside of any objects you draw.

The linesize box below the toolbar identifies the width of a line and the options for the currently selected tool in the toolbox. Depending on which tool is selected, you might use the linesize box to determine how wide of a line the line tool draws, how wide the eraser is, whether a shape is filled or transparent, and so on. Table 14.1 shows each of the tools in the toolbox.

TABLE 14.1   TOOLS IN THE PAINT TOOLBOX

TOOL	NAME
	Free-Form Select
	Select
	Eraser/Color Eraser
	Fill with Color
	Pick Color
	Magnifier

TOOL	NAME
	Pencil
	Brush
	Airbrush
	Text
	Line
	Curve
	Rectangle
	Polygon
	Ellipse
	Rounded Rectangle

DRAWING IN PAINT

Drawing is somewhat difficult in Paint, but practice always makes a difference. You use your mouse to draw lines, curves, and shapes, as well as to enter text in Paint.

Follow these steps to draw:

1. To select the fill color, right-click any color in the palette.

2. To select the line color, click any color in the palette.

3. To select the size of the drawing, choose Image, Attributes and enter the Width and Height in the Attributes dialog box (see Figure 14.2). Click OK. The new size is defined by eight small black handles or boxes, outlining the specified area.

FIGURE 14.2   Choose the size of the drawing before you begin drawing.

4. Click a drawing tool in the toolbox at the left of the screen.

5. To select a line width for any line tool—line, curve, rectangle, ellipse, and so on—click the line size you want in the line size box in the lower-left corner of the screen.

Which Tool?   Try starting with either the rectangle tool, the ellipse tool, or the straight line tool to experiment. Then branch out to the other tools as you learn more about the program.

6. To draw an object, point at the area where you want the object to appear (within the boxed Image area), press and hold the left mouse button, and drag the mouse pointer until the object is the size you want.

Oops!   If you add to your graphic and then decide you don't like the addition, choose Edit, Undo (or press Ctrl+Z) to undo the change you made.

TIP   **A Perfect Circle Every Time**   To draw a perfect circle, select the Ellipse tool, hold down the Shift key, and click and drag the mouse pointer. You can also use this technique to draw a perfect square with the Rectangle tool or a perfectly straight line with the Line tool.

ADDING TEXT TO A GRAPHIC

Using the Text tool, you can add text to a graphic such as a logo or illustration. To add text to a graphic, follow these steps:

1. Select the Text tool.

2. Drag the text tool to create a rectangle in which you will type the text. A rectangle that will hold the text and an insertion point appear.

3. Before you type, choose View, Text Toolbar. The Fonts toolbar appears, as shown in Figure 14.3. Choose the font, size, and attributes from the Fonts toolbar.

4. Click the insertion point within the rectangle and type your text, pressing Enter at the end of each line. When you finish typing the text, choose another tool from the toolbox or click the next place you want to insert a new line of text. If you want to make a change to the formatting of the text, select the text and use the Font toolbar.

5. Click outside of the text box anywhere to accept the text you just entered.

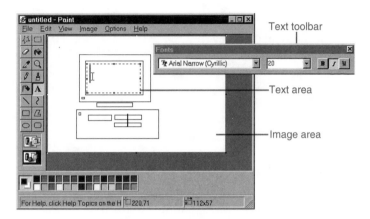

FIGURE 14.3   Use Paint's tools to create a company logo.

 Once You Leave, You Can Never Get Back   You can't edit or reformat text once you've accepted it; you can only erase it. To erase the text, click the Select tool, draw a frame around the text and choose Edit, Cut. (This also works for any lines or shapes you want to erase.) Be careful when cutting, however; you can cut out parts of shapes and text and leave other parts intact.

 Move or Size Object   To move the text (or any other part of the drawing), select it with the Select tool and then drag it to a new position. To resize an object, select it and then position the mouse pointer over one of the handles around the selection rectangle. Drag the two-headed arrow to change the size of the text or object.

Figure 14.4 shows a logo using graphics and text created in Paint, with the text selected and ready to move.

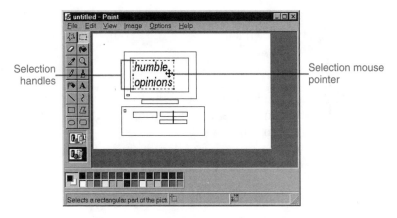

FIGURE 14.4   Create a company logo.

SAVING THE DRAWING

Most likely, you will want to save your drawing so that you can use it again; you might want to use it in a WordPad document, for example.

To save a drawing, follow these steps:

1. Choose File, Save As. The Save As dialog box appears.

2. If you want to change the file type, choose a file type from the Save as Type drop-down list box.

3. In the Save In drop-down box choose a drive in which to save the file.

4. In the list box, double-click the folder to which you want to save the file.

5. In the **File Name** box, enter a name for the file. Choose **Save** and Paint saves the file.

6. To close Paint, click the Close button or choose File, Exit.

Want to Print it?   To learn how to print in Windows programs, see Lesson 15.

In this lesson, you learned to open the Paint program, create a drawing with Paint, and save the drawing. In the next lesson, you learn to Print with Windows 95.

PRINTING WITH WINDOWS 95

In this lesson, you learn to print from an application, control the print job, and connect to a network printer.

INSTALLING A PRINTER

You can easily install a printer to work with all of your Windows applications. Windows includes many *drivers* for various manufacturers' computers. To install a printer, you'll need your Windows CD-ROM or a disk containing printer drivers that came with your printer.

> **Printer Drivers** Printer drivers are software programs you install to your computer. The drivers make the printer work with Windows 95 and your Windows applications.

To install a printer, follow these steps:

1. Choose the Start button, and then click Settings, Printers. The Printers window appears.

2. Double-click the Add Printer icon to display the Add Printer Wizard dialog box. Click Next to begin installing a new printer.

3. Choose whether to install a local printer or a network printer and then choose the Next button.

Local or Network Printer? A local printer is one connected directly to your computer; a network printer is one that may be connected to another computer on the network and is used by several workstations in addition to yours.

4. In the third Add Printer Wizard dialog box, choose the Manufacturer of your printer, such as Hewlett Packard, and then the model of the printer, such as Laserjet 4 Plus, as shown in Figure 15.1.

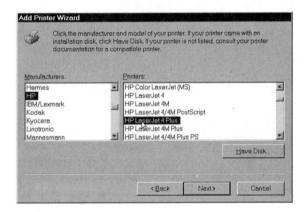

FIGURE 15.1 Choose the printer you want to install.

5. If you have a disk from the printer's manufacturer that contains Windows 95 drivers, insert the disk in the disk drive and click the Have Disk button; alternatively, insert your Windows 95 Setup CD-ROM and click the Next button.

6. Follow the directions on-screen. When Windows finishes setting up the printer, it returns to the Printers window.

PRINTING FROM AN APPLICATION

The steps for printing from any Windows application are very similar. The biggest difference is that some dialog box options change from program to program. Most programs offer a Print icon on the toolbar that you can click to print one copy of the job; although in some programs, the print icon displays the Print dialog box. To print from a Windows application, follow these steps:

1. Choose File, Print, and the Print dialog box appears. Figure 15.2 shows the Print dialog box in the WordPad accessory program.

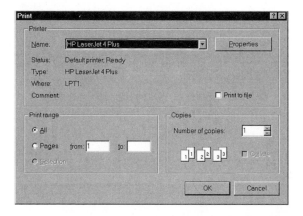

FIGURE 15.2   Use the Print dialog box to specify printing options.

2. Set any of the printing options described in the following list. (Some applications will offer more specialized options; see a particular application's Help feature if you have questions):

    • **Print Range**   Specify the pages you want to print. For example, you can print all pages, the current page, a range of pages, or a selection of text (which you select before opening the Print dialog box.)

- **Copies** Enter the number of copies to print. Often, you can choose a print order (front to back, for example) and whether to collate the copies or not.

- **Print to File** Prints the document into a file, which you can use to print your document from a computer that doesn't have the program you used to create it. (You then print the file by typing **print filename** at the DOS prompt of any computer. All document formatting is preserved.)

- **Printer** If you have several printers available, you can choose the printer to which you want to send the job.

- **Properties or Setup** Usually leads to a dialog box in which you can set paper size, orientation, paper tray, graphics resolution, and other options specific to your printer.

- **Collate Copies** Assembles the copies of a multiple-page document in order from 1, to 2, to 3, and so on.

3. When you're ready to print, choose OK. Windows sends the job to the printer.

Printing Errors If your job doesn't print and you receive an error message from Windows, check to see that the printer is on and there is paper in it. Next, jiggle the cable at the printer's end and again at the computer's end, to make sure the cable is not loose. Try printing again.

Print Job A print job is a document you're printing. Each time you choose OK in the Print dialog box, you're sending a print job to the printer (whether that document contains one page or forty).

WORKING WITH THE PRINT FOLDER

When you print a document, the printer usually begins processing the job immediately. But what if the printer is working on another job that you (or someone else, if you're working on a network printer) sent? When that happens, there is a print queue that holds the job until the printer is ready for it.

 Print Queue   A holding area for jobs waiting to be printed. If you were to open the contents of the queue, the jobs would appear in the order they were sent to the printer.

You can check the status of a print job you've sent by looking at the Print queue, found in the Printer's folder. Figure 15.3 shows a document in the Print queue. As you can see, the print queue window displays the information about the job.

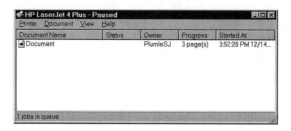

FIGURE 15.3   Use the Print queue to track your print jobs.

To display the Print queue, follow these steps:

1. From the Desktop, choose the Start button and then choose Settings, and Printers.

2. In the Printers folder, double-click the icon of the printer to which you are printing.

Empty Print Queue?   If no jobs appear in the Print queue, the job has already been sent to the printer.

Controlling the Print Job

It's hard to control just one or two jobs because they usually go to the printer too quickly. However, if there are several jobs in the print queue, you can control them. For example, you can pause and resume print jobs and you can delete a job before it prints.

Additionally, you can control the printer or just one particular document. You can, for example, cancel one document or all documents in the queue.

Pausing and Resuming the Queue

You may want to pause the queue and then resume printing later if, for example, the paper in the printer is misaligned or the printer is using the wrong color paper. Pausing the print queue gives you time to correct the problem. To pause the print queue, choose Printer, Pause Printing. To resume printing, choose Printer, Pause Printing a second time to remove the check mark beside the command.

 Printer Stalled   If your printer stalls while it's processing your print job, Windows displays the word "stalled" in the printer status line in the queue. Choose Printer, Pause Printing to remove the check mark from the command and start printing again. If the printer stalls again, see if there's a problem with the printer (it might be offline or out of paper, for example).

Deleting a Print Job

Sometimes you'll send a document to the printer and then change your mind. For example, you may think of additional text to add to a document or realize you forgot to check your spelling. In such a case, deleting the print job is easy, if you can catch it in time. Follow these steps:

1. Open the Print queue by choosing Start, Settings, and Printers; double-click the printer icon.

2. Select the job you want to delete.

3. Choose Document, Cancel.

 Clear the Queue!   To remove all files from the print queue, choose Purge Print Jobs.

In this lesson, you learned to print from an application, control the print job, and connect to a network printer. In the next lesson, you learn to use the My Computer window.

LESSON

VIEWING YOUR COMPUTER

In this lesson, you learn to open the My Computer window, view the contents of your computer, and open folders and change options.

OPENING THE MY COMPUTER WINDOW

The My Computer icon on your desktop represents the contents and components of your computer, including the hard drive and all of the folders and files on it. You may also see floppy drives (a: or b:), CD-ROM drives, tape backups (d:-or higher), and other peripherals connected to your computer as well as the Control Panel and Printers folders. If your computer is equipped with remote access capabilities, you'll also see the DialUp folder.

Peripherals Peripherals include any hardware connected to your computer, such as printers, modems, CD-ROM drives, and so on.

To open the My Computer window, double-click the icon. Figure 16.1 shows common components of a My Computer window.

Use the Familiar Window Elements You can use the toolbar, menu, Maximize and Minimize buttons, and other common window elements in the My Computer window just as you would in any window.

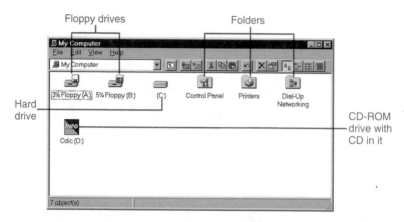

Figure 16.1   View the components of your computer.

TIP   **Rename My Computer**   If you want to, you can rename the My Computer icon and window to any name you like. On the desktop, select My Computer by clicking it once, then click the text once more. The text changes to a rename box and the mouse pointer changes to an I-beam. Type the new name and press Enter to accept it.

Viewing the Contents of a Drive

You can view the contents of any drive—hard drive, floppy, CD-ROM, and so on— by opening the icon in the My Computer window. When you open a drive icon, a separate window appears displaying the contents of that drive.

To view the contents of a drive, double-click the drive icon. Figure 16.2 shows a hard drive window and all of its contents.

If you want, you can choose to show the toolbar in any window by selecting View, Toolbar. A check mark appears beside the command and the toolbar displays. Use the toolbar to change the view of the contents of the window.

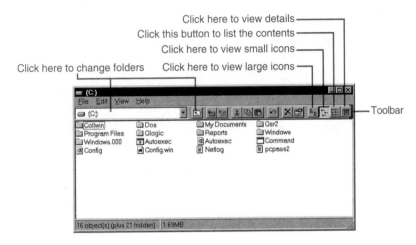

FIGURE 16.2 Open any of the drive icons to view its contents.

Using toolbar buttons, you can change your view of the window's contents. For example, click the first button on the toolbar to change drives; you can view a floppy drive, CD-ROM drive, or folders on your computer using this drop-down list.

You also can click a button on the toolbar (refer to Figure 16.2) to change how you view the contents of the window. The default view is small icons but you can change the view to large icons, a list of folders and files, or to a detailed view that shows the file name, modification date, and the file type and size (see Figure 16.3).

FIGURE 16.3 View the details of a drive.

> **Use the Menu Instead** You can choose the View menu and then select the Large Icons, Small Icons, List, or Details command to change views of the window, if you would rather use the menu instead of the toolbar buttons.

MANAGING FOLDERS AND FILES

You can use the My Computer window to perform any of the tasks you perform in the Explorer—including creating and deleting files and folders, moving, copying, and renaming files and folders, and so on. See Lessons 9, 10, and 11 for more information.

You open a folder in the My Computer window by double-clicking it; a window appears, displaying that window's contents. You can resize, minimize, move, close, and otherwise manipulate the window as well as show the toolbar and view the window's contents in different ways:

- To create a new folder in the window, choose File, New, Folder. Name the folder and press Enter.

- To rename a file or folder, select the file or folder and choose File, Rename. Type the new name and press Enter.

- To delete a file or folder, select it and choose File, Delete. Click the Yes button to confirm the deletion.

- To copy or move a file or folder, select the item and choose Edit, Cut or Copy. Open the folder or drive you want to copy the selected item to and choose Edit, Paste.

- To close the folder's window, click the Close button (X) or choose File, Close.

CHANGING OPTIONS

When you use the My Computer window to manage and view files and folders, Windows opens a new window for every folder you open. The Windows Explorer, on the other hand, uses only one window for viewing each successive open folder. You can change the number of windows you open from the My Computer window by changing options.

To change the My Computer window's options, follow these steps:

1. Open the My Computer window.

2. Choose View, Options. The Options dialog box appears (see Figure 16.4).

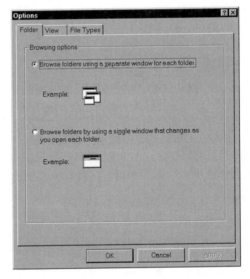

FIGURE 16.4 Change the options for the My Computer window.

3. Choose the Folder tab, if it is not already selected, and then click the Browse folders by using a single window that changes as you open each folder option.

4. Choose OK to close the dialog box.

Show Those Hidden Files   Sometimes you need to see all files in a directory, including hidden and system files. By default, Windows hides certain files from you so you won't accidentally delete or move them; Windows needs these files to operate properly. If, however, you need to see the hidden or system files on your computer, you can choose to show those files in the Options dialog box. Open the dialog box (View, Options) and choose the View tab. In the Hidden files area, choose Show All Files. Choose OK to close the dialog box.

Note: there is also an application called the Windows Explorer (which will be described later) you can use to perform many of the following tasks; the Explorer is similar to the Windows 3.x File Manager.

When you're finished with the My Computer window, close the window by clicking the Close button (X).

In this lesson, you learned to open the My Computer window, view the contents of your computer, and open folders and change options. In the next lesson, you learn to use the MS-DOS Prompt.

L E S S O N

17

USING THE MS-DOS PROMPT

In this lesson, you learn to open a MS-DOS window, use commands, install a DOS application, and close the MS-DOS window.

WHAT IS THE MS-DOS PROMPT?

The MS-DOS prompt is a character-based interface to Windows 95: You can type in commands at a prompt to perform tasks, to run applications, and to otherwise control the computer, your files and directories, and your programs.

Use the MS-DOS prompt to perform the following operations:

- Start and work with applications that are DOS-based.

- Issue commands, including directory listing, file management, and configuration commands.

- Share data between DOS-based applications.

Prompt   The MS-DOS prompt in Windows does not truly use a DOS you're familiar with. If you type **ver** (version) at the prompt, for example, the following appears: Windows 95 (Version 4.00.1111). You can, however, use many of the familiar DOS commands you've used in the past and you can open and run many DOS applications as you would from a regular DOS prompt.

Prompt When I refer to a prompt, DOS prompt, or command prompt, I'm referring to the text you see in the MS-DOS Prompt window, such as C:\ or C:\WINDOWS.

OPENING A DOS WINDOW

You can open and close a DOS window to perform various tasks. You can even open more than one DOS window at a time, if necessary. When you're finished with a DOS window, you should close it to spare your system's resources and memory.

Running in DOS? If you have several open DOS windows, each with its own application running, your computer may slow down because of the drain on your system's resources. Running DOS applications in Windows 95 is sometimes possible but not always practical, depending on the application.

To start and quit an MS-DOS window, follow these steps:

1. From the Desktop, choose the Start button. Select Programs and then choose MS-DOS Prompt. The MS-DOS Prompt window appears. As you can see in Figure 17.1, the default prompt is the Windows.000 drive and directory.

2. When you're ready to quit the command prompt, exit all applications (using each application's quit or exit command). Then type **exit** at the prompt and press Enter. You can, alternatively, use the window's Close button (X).

Control
menu
button

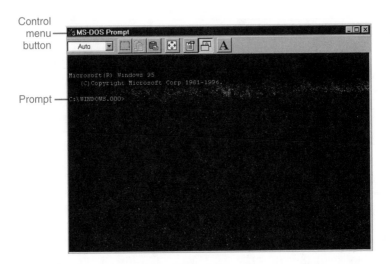

Prompt

FIGURE 17.1   The MS-DOS Prompt window.

It's Just Another Window   Notice the MS-DOS prompt
window has all of the elements of any window: Minimize
and Maximize buttons, title bar, borders, toolbar, and so
on.

Restarting the Computer in MS-DOS Mode   As an
alternative to running the DOS prompt in a window, you
can shut down the computer and choose to run in MS-
DOS Mode, meaning you do not have the advantages of
opening and switching between windows. To shut down
the computer, choose Start, Shut Down. In the Shut Down
Windows dialog box, choose Restart the Computer in MS-
DOS Mode and choose Yes. To return to Windows from
MS-DOS mode, type **exit** or **win** at the DOS prompt.

Using Commands

There are hundreds of commands you can use at the DOS prompt and if you have questions about any of them, you should use the Help feature, as described in the next section. If you already know the DOS operating system, you can use many of the DOS commands you're used to; some commands, however, will not work in this version of Windows 95 DOS.

Before I tell you about specific commands, let me tell you about a few things that relate to all commands. Syntax is the order in which you must type the command and any additional elements (command name, parameters, switches, and/or values) that follow it. A parameter is information that defines the object upon which you're performing a command, and a switch modifies how the command is performed. In the command **dir *.doc /s**, for example, **dir** is the command, ***.doc** is the parameter, and **/s** is the switch. This command tells Windows to list a directory of all documents with a DOC extension found in all subdirectories of the current directory, or folder.

Table 17.1 lists a few of the more common commands.

TABLE 17.1   COMMON COMMANDS

COMMAND	PARAMETER	FUNCTION
break		Stops the previous command
cd\		Changes to the root directory
cd	*subdirectory*	Changes to the specified subdirectory
cls		Clears the screen
copy	*filename drive\directory*	Copies the specified file to the specified drive and /or directory

continues

TABLE 17.1   CONTINUED

COMMAND	PARAMETER	FUNCTION
dir		Displays a list of files and subdirectories in the current directory
erase	*file(s)*	Deletes one or more specified file(s); you should separate each file with a space
move	*filename drive\directory*	Moves the specified file to the specified drive and/or directory
ren	*oldfilename newfilename*	Renames the file specified by *oldfilename* with the name specified by *newfilename*
start		Starts a separate window in which to run a command or program
edit		Starts the MS-DOS Editor, in which you can create and edit text files
exit		Closes the MS-DOS Prompt window

To use a command, first open the MS-DOS window. Type the command and any additional parameters or switches at the command prompt and press Enter. Figure 17.2 shows the MS-DOS window with the results of the command dir*., which displays a list of directories only, no files.

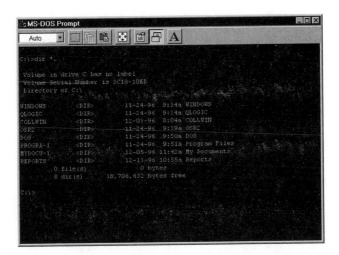

FIGURE 17.2   The dir*. command offers many parameters and switches that enable you to display the directories on your computer.

TIP

Slow Down!   When you list a directory, it usually scrolls by so quickly that you can't read everything on the list. To fix that, type a slash p (**dir /p**) after the command. The /p stands for "pause," which tells Windows to pause the listing a screen at a time so you can see everything in the list. When the list is paused, you can press any key to continue to the next screen.

Error Message   If, after entering a command, you receive a message that says the name specified is not recognized, you may have misspelled the command or used the wrong parameters. Try entering the command again. If you continue to have problems, check the online Help system, which you'll learn about next.

GETTING HELP

Just as you can get online Help by using the commands in the Windows Help menu, you can get online help for all commands at the command prompt. Table 17.2 describes the common Help commands you can type at the prompt.

TABLE 17.2   HELP COMMANDS

COMMAND	FORM OF HELP PROVIDED
command/?	Gives you help on the syntax, parameters, and switches for the command you enter (for example, if you type **dir /?**, it gives you help on the **dir** command)
net help	Lists the names and descriptions of network commands
net help *command*	Lists the syntax, parameters, and switches for network commands

INSTALLING A DOS APPLICATION

You can install a DOS application to Windows 95 and run the application in the MS-DOS Prompt window. The command you use to start the installation will depend on the application you're installing. Refer to the documentation that came with the application before installing it.

To install a DOS application, follow these steps:

1. Insert the diskette or CD in the appropriate drive.

2. Choose Start, Programs, MS-DOS Prompt.

3. At the prompt, type the drive letter in which the installation disk appears; for example, type **a:** or **d:** and the name of the installation program, as outlined in your application's documentation. You might, for instance, type **a:\install.exe** or **d:\setup.exe.**

4. Press Enter and follow any directions on-screen. When you're done, remove the disk from the drive. If you have any problems during installation, refer to the application's documentation.

RUNNING APPLICATIONS IN THE MS-DOS PROMPT WINDOW

You can run MS-DOS applications from the DOS prompt in a window or by restarting the computer in MS-DOS mode, as described earlier. To run a program from the command prompt, follow these steps:

1. From the Desktop, open the Start menu; choose Programs and then choose the MS-DOS Prompt. The DOS prompt window appears.

2. If necessary, use the cd command to change to the directory holding the program you want to start. For example, to change to the WordPerfect directory, you'd type **cd\wp60** and press Enter.

TIP

What Directory?   You may not need to change to the application's directory to start the program; to find out if you do, type **cd** to change to the root directory (C:) and then type the application's name. If it starts, you won't have to worry about the directory; if you get an error message, go to step 2 above.

3. At the prompt, enter the program name that starts the program (for example, you'd type **wp** to start WordPerfect).

My Games Won't Run in the DOS Window! If you have trouble running any DOS applications (especially some games) in an MS-DOS Prompt window, try rebooting the computer in MS-DOS Mode and running the application from there.

 Copy and Paste Between Applications You can take advantage of the Windows Clipboard even in DOS applications. In your DOS program, select the text or graphic you want to copy and then click the MS-DOS Prompt window Control menu button. Choose Edit, Copy. Switch to another application—DOS or Windows—position the insertion point, and choose Edit, Paste.

When you're done with a DOS application, make sure you close and save all documents and then exit the program according to the application's directions. Then type **exit** to close the DOS window.

CLOSING THE MS-DOS PROMPT WINDOW

When you're done with the DOS window, you should close it to conserve system resources. There are several methods to closing the window, as described in the following list:

- Type **exit** and press Enter.
- Click the Close button (X).
- Click the Control menu button and choose Close.

In this lesson, you learned to open an MS-DOS window, use commands, install a DOS application, and close the MS-DOS window. In the next lesson, you learn to connect to and view a network drive.

VIEWING A NETWORK DRIVE

In this lesson, you learn to open the Network Neighborhood and view a network drive.

WHAT IS A NETWORK?

Most networks consist of servers and clients, although some consist solely of workstations (called "peer-to-peer" networks.) Windows 95 is a client that can attach and share data with various servers—Windows NT, Novell NetWare, Microsoft LAN Manager, for example— and with a peer-to-peer network, such as Windows 95, LANtastic, or Windows for Workgroups.

When you connect to a network, you gain certain advantages:

- Access to shared resources, such as modems and printers.

- Access to shared data, such as files and directories.

- The capability to send and receive messages with others on the network using a mail program.

- The capability to back up your files to the server (see your system administrator for more information).

System Administrator The system or network administrator is the person who oversees your network. The administrator can grant a user permission to access certain files and resources, troubleshoot problems with the network, and control each computer on the network.

Client/Server A client/server network is one in which the workstation computer logs on to and attaches to a server that controls shared files, printers, and other resources.

Peer-to-peer A peer-to-peer network is one in which all workstations are connected and each can share its printer, files, folders, and other resources.

Workstation Any computer that is attached to a network for the purposes of using the network resources. A workstation computer can run Windows 95, DOS, Windows 3.1, Windows NT, and other operating systems.

Using a User Name and Password

You know that to gain access to Windows, you must enter your user name and password, which identify you to the computer, and to the network, if you are attached to one. The user name that appears when you log on to Windows and the password you enter are those that you or the system administrator created. These devices provide security not only for your work, but for the entire network. Therefore, someone who does not know his or her user name and password cannot log on to the network.

Log On To connect to a network, you must log on. When you log on, you're essentially telling the network that you're ready to share its resources. The network uses your logon as a key, of sorts, to identify which resources you may use.

Windows keeps a record of any applications you install, shortcuts you create, and any colors, fonts, display, or other settings you modify on the desktop. When you log on using your user name and password, Windows displays those settings individual to you. If you logged on under a different name or just canceled the dialog box, your individual customizations would not appear when Windows opened.

OPENING THE NETWORK NEIGHBORHOOD

When you connect to a network drive, you add a whole new set of folders, and files—not to mention other resources—to your working environment. After connecting, you can remain connected to the network while you work, or if you need to access something else, you can disconnect from the network and connect again at any time. (You might, for example, disconnect from one server to attach to another server.)

To open the Network Neighborhood and view your network connections, follow these steps:

1. From the desktop, double-click the Network Neighborhood icon to open that window. Figure 18.1 shows the Network Neighborhood window displaying the Humble server of an NT Network to which the Windows 95 computer is attached. Depending on the network you're attached to, your Network Neighborhood may look different, but the theory and procedures are the same.

2. If you do not see your network in the Network Neighborhood window, double-click the Entire Network icon. The Entire Network window opens, displaying the networks and/or domains available to you.

3. Double-click any server or other computer listed in your Network Neighborhood window to see what resources are available to you. A list of printers, files, folders, or other peripherals may appear.

Don't Panic!   If you cannot access a network drive, don't worry. The server might be down for repair, a cable might have come loose, you may not have permission to view other computers, or some other problem might have occurred. All of these problems can easily be solved by seeing your system administrator.

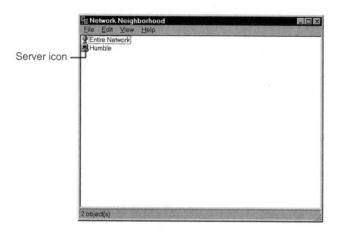

Server icon

FIGURE 18.1 You can access any available network and even connect to multiple networks.

ACCESSING SHARED RESOURCES

You can display files or other resources on the network drive in either the Network Neighborhood or the Explorer; either way, you can treat the files and folders just as you would any files on your own hard drive. To open any server, computer, or other resource, simply double-click the icon representing the resource; as long as you see folders and files, you have permission to use those items.

Figure 18.2 shows the stepped windows for a peer-to-peer network. The first window shows the Entire Network icon and the Humble server on an NT network. Instead of accessing the server, I double-clicked the Entire Network icon to reveal two domains: Opinions and Workgroup, Workgroup being a peer-to-peer connection between Windows computers. When I opened the Workgroup icon, two computers appeared and when I opened one of the computers, its hard drive appeared. Finally, I opened the hard drive to see the folders available to me over the network.

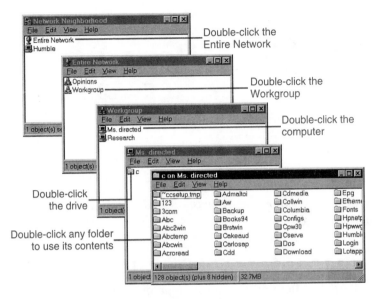

FIGURE 18.2   Access data and resources over the network.

In this lesson, you learned to open the Network Neighborhood and view a network drive. In the next lesson, you learn to send and receive network mail.

19 SENDING AND RECEIVING NETWORK MAIL

In this lesson, you learn how to use the Inbox, send and receive messages over the network, delete messages, and set options in the mail program.

WHAT IS NETWORK MAIL?

You use the Microsoft Exchange program to send and receive mail messages within your LAN (local area network). Using the mail program, you can send and receive messages to anyone else who is attached to your network and can attach files—such as reports, memos, spreadsheets, and so on—to any message you send over the network.

The mail program is called Windows Messaging in Windows 95 and is represented by the Inbox icon on the desktop. Microsoft Exchange is the means by which the messaging operates.

The messages you send and receive all go to one main post office set up on the network server by the network administrator. When you open the mail program on your computer, Microsoft Exchange automatically checks your mail box on the server and delivers any mail you have waiting to your Inbox.

Your Inbox may or may not be configured and ready to go. When you first start the mail program, the Microsoft Exchange Setup Wizard will appear if your mail program is not configured. You'll need to create a profile by entering your name, post office on the server (directory), password, and other information. If you need help setting the profile, contact your network or mail administrator.

Network Administrator   Also called a system administrator, this is the person who manages the network by setting up the server, printers, post office, workstations, applications, and other resources dealing with the network. Additionally, a very large network may employ a specialized Mail Administrator who handles only that portion of network resources.

After the Inbox is set up, you can use it to send and receive messages, delete and print messages, and set options for more efficient mail handling. The following steps walk you through starting and exiting the mail program.

1. From the Desktop, choose the Start button, Programs, and Windows Messaging; alternatively, double-click the Inbox.

No Windows Messaging or Inbox?   If you do not see either the command or the Inbox in Windows, you'll need to install the application from the Windows Setup on the network or on a Windows 95 CD. In the Control Panel, double-click Add/Remove Programs and select the Windows Setup tab. Double-click Windows Messaging in the Components list and check Microsoft Mail Services and Windows Messaging. Choose OK and OK again. Follow the directions on-screen.

2. If you've opened the program before, the Windows Messaging window appears (see Figure 19.1). The program opens to the same folder that was open the last time you used it (the folder's name appears in the title bar).

3. To exit the program, choose File, Exit.

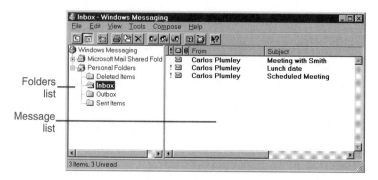

Folders list

Message list

FIGURE 19.1 Use the Windows Messaging program to send and receive e-mail.

USING FOLDERS

The Windows Messaging window opens with several folders displaying in the folder list. When you select the folder in the left pane, its contents appear in the right pane, or message list. The program supplies you with a set of Personal folders; you may also see shared folders in the folder list that your network administrator has designated for your use.

You can open any folder by clicking it once. You also can drag any message from the right pane to a different folder in the left pane. Following is a description of each of the Personal folders.

- The Inbox displays all mail you've received and retains that mail until you delete it or store it in another folder. You can open messages and read them, delete messages, and send messages from the Inbox.

- The Deleted Items folder contains any messages that you've deleted. You can move messages to the Deleted Items folder as well as out of the folder, if you change your mind about deleting something.

- The Outbox holds any mail items you are about to send. You can store, for example, unfinished messages here or messages written while you were not connected to the network.

- The Sent Items folder contains a copy of all e-mail messages you send for reference, printing, or resending.

You can create a new folder—say to hold special correspondence, reports, personal e-mail, and so on—and store any mail you want in that folder.

To create a new folder, follow these steps:

1. Select the folder you want to contain the new folder, for example, select Personal Folders if you want to add a folder on the same level as the Inbox, Outbox, Deleted Items, and Sent Items.

2. Choose File, New Folder. The New Folder dialog box appears.

3. Enter the name of the new folder in the text box and choose OK.

To delete a folder, select it and press the Delete key. Windows doesn't warn you about the deletion or display a confirmation dialog box.

SENDING AND RECEIVING MESSAGES

You can compose a message, address it, send a carbon copy of it, and specify other options in the Mail program. In addition, you can read and respond to messages you receive.

To create and send a message, follow these steps:

1. Choose Compose, New Message. The New Message window appears (see Figure 19.2).

2. In the To text box, enter the name of the person you want to send the message to; alternatively, click the To button and choose the name from the list of names in the Address Book.

3. Optionally, enter one or more names in the Cc text box. You can enter multiple names by separating them with a semi-colon.

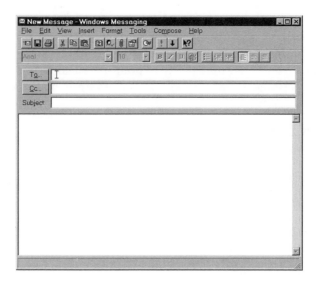

Figure 19.2 Compose a new message to someone on your network.

4. In the Subject text box enter a title for the message.

5. In the message area, type your message. You are not limited to the space you see. As you type, the message scrolls upward in the box so you can fit more text in the message area.

6. Choose File, Send to send the message.

You can format the text in a message by selecting the text and choosing the Format menu, and then Font or Paragraph; alternatively, use the formatting toolbar. Display the toolbar by choosing View, Formatting Toolbar.

New mail is displayed in your Inbox in bold type. After you read the message, the type is regular as opposed to bold. To read a message you've received, follow these steps:

1. In the Windows Messaging program window, click the Inbox folder to display a list of received messages.

2. Double-click any message to read it.

3. To reply to the message, choose Compose, Reply to Sender. Type your reply and choose File, Send.

Deliver Right Now Your mail program periodically connects to the network and sends and receives messages; however, if you don't want to wait, you can choose Tools, Deliver Now to send all messages you've composed and stored in the Outbox. For more information about automatic mail delivery, see the section, "Setting Options."

DELETING MESSAGES

In order to keep your messages from piling up, you should delete a message when you no longer need it. You can delete a message you've read by choosing File, Delete. In addition, you can delete any message from the message list by dragging it to the Deleted Items folder.

If you change your mind and want the deleted message back, open the Deleted Items folder and select the message. Drag the selected message to another folder. If any messages remain in the Deleted Items folder when you exit the program, those messages are deleted permanently.

SETTING OPTIONS

Windows Messaging provides several options you can set to customize the program. You'll want to make the program suit your mail needs and preferences.

To change program options, follow these steps:

1. In the Windows Messaging window, choose Tools, Options. The Options dialog box appears (see Figure 19.3).

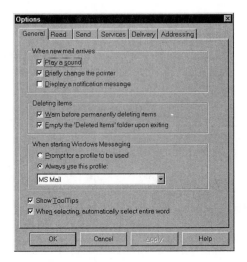

Figure 19.3　Change mail options to suit yourself.

2. In the **General** tab, choose how you want to be notified of new mail, deletion options, and which profile to use when starting the program.

3. In the **Read** tab, specify options for how the program deals with open items and forwarded items.

4. In the **Send** tab, specify options for sending mail, such as the font used, receipt requests, importance levels of the message, and so on.

5. Use the **Services** tab to add, remove, copy, and view properties of your mail services, including post office path, address book configuration, and so on.

6. In the **Delivery** tab, specify a location for new mail and the order in which your information services are accessed.

7. Use the **Addressing** tab to control the post office and personal address lists.

8. Choose OK to accept the changes.

In this lesson, you learned how to use the Inbox, send and receive messages over the network, delete messages, and set options in the mail program. In the next lesson, you learn to use the Internet Explorer.

USING
INTERNET
EXPLORER

*In this lesson, you learn how to use
Internet Explorer to browse the Internet.*

ACCESSING THE INTERNET

Windows comes with Internet Explorer 3.0 that you can use for
browsing the World Wide Web. Internet Explorer enables you to
access Web pages, download files, perform searches on the Net,
and more. The browser displays pages complete with images,
links, and text. This lesson assumes your Internet is set up and
ready to go.

Browser Any software you use to view the Internet; in
this case, Internet Explorer.

Download Transferring a file from the Internet to your
own computer.

Links Also called Hyperlinks, links are underlined text
on Web pages that jump to other Web pages containing
related information.

Set Up? Help! In order to use Internet Explorer, you
must have a connection through an Internet Service Provider and a modem attached to your computer or over the
network. See Appendix A for information about configuring your computer for the Internet.

To start Internet Explorer, follow these steps:

1. Choose Start, Programs, Internet Explorer; alternatively, you can double-click the Internet icon on the desktop.

2. The Connect To dialog box appears (see Figure 20.1). Choose Connect to dial and connect to the Internet. Explorer dials your Internet Service Provider (ISP) and then displays the Internet Explorer window and the Microsoft home page.

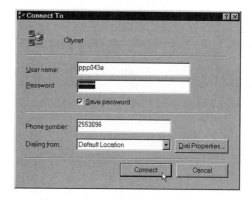

FIGURE 20.1 Choose to connect to the Internet.

Internet Service Provider A vendor who provides you with a phone number you can use to connect to the Internet. The ISP also provides addresses and other information you'll need to configure the computer for the Internet.

Microsoft Home Page The first Web site you see after connecting to the Internet is the Microsoft Home Page, a Web page that tells you about Microsoft as well as other services you can access over the Net.

USING INTERNET EXPLORER

Internet Explorer opens to the Microsoft Home Page. You can use your mouse to scroll around the page and view the contents. When you see any underlined text, or the mouse pointer changes to a hand, you can click that link to see more, related information on a subject. For example, click Today's Link (see Figure 20.2) to view a link to another site that you may be interested in; this week, the link is to Hallmark's home page but the link changes from time to time, as do many links on the Web.

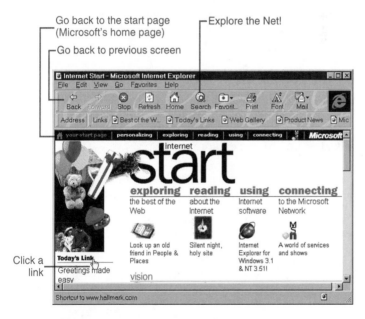

FIGURE 20.2   Surf the Web.

If you go to a link but want to return to the previous page, click the Back button on the toolbar.

SEARCHING THE NET

You can quickly find Web pages about any topic by searching for the topic. Internet Explorer provides several different search types you can use and experiment with.

To search for a specific topic on the Internet, follow these steps:

1. Choose Go, Search the Web; alternatively, click the Search button on the toolbar.

2. In the Search text box, enter the word or phrase for which you're searching.

3. Click the Search button.

TIP **Explore the Search Page**   Scroll through the search page and see what other types of searching are available on the Web. Experiment!

4. The results of the search appear on-screen; you can scroll the page to see the topics found and click any underlined topic to view more information about it. Click the **Back** button to return to the Internet Searches page or choose link after link to just explore the Net.

SAVING FAVORITE PLACES

You'll likely find Web sites that you will want to visit again. You can save the addresses to these sites so you can quickly go to them in the future.

To save a Web site to your Favorites folder, follow these steps:

1. While at the actual site, click the Favorites button on the toolbar to display the Favorites menu (see Figure 20.3).

2. Select the Add To Favorites command and the Internet Explorer displays the Add to Favorites dialog box.

3. You can enter an alternate name in the Name text box to represent the site or you can accept the default name supplied. Choose OK and the site is added to your Favorites menu.

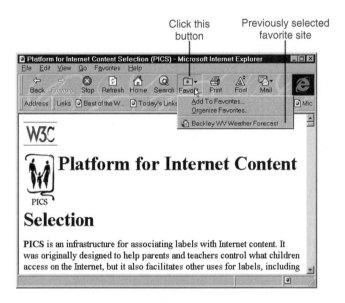

FIGURE 20.3   Create a menu of all your favorite places on the Web.

To access any of your favorite places, choose Favorites, Open Favorites, and select the site from the menu.

GOING TO A SPECIFIC SITE

If you know the address of the Web site you want to visit, you can enter the address and go directly to that site. Follow these steps:

1. If the Address bar is not showing, click the Address button below the toolbar (refer to figure 20.3).

2. Enter the address in the Address text box and press Enter. The addresses you visit during one session are listed in the drop-down address list so you can go back to any of the listings at any time during the session.

Exiting the Program

When you're done surfing the Web and you're ready to close Internet Explorer, you can remain connected or you can disconnect from the Internet. If you remain connected, you can access Internet Mail or Internet News, as explained in the next two lessons. If you're finished with the Internet, you must use the Dial-Up Networking folder to disconnect.

1. To exit Internet Explorer, choose File, Exit. If the Disconnect dialog box appears, confirming you want to disconnect from the Internet, choose Yes to disconnect or No to continue the session with Internet Mail or Internet News.

2. If the Disconnect dialog box doesn't appear, open the Computer window and double-click the Dial-Up Networking icon. The Dial-Up Networking dialog box appears. Select your current connection and choose File, Disconnect. Close the open windows.

In this lesson, you learned how to use Internet Explorer to browse the Internet. In the next lesson, you learn to use Internet Mail.

USING INTERNET MAIL

In this lesson, you learn how to open and close the Internet Mail program, read and reply to mail, and create mail.

WHAT IS INTERNET MAIL?

Internet Mail is an e-mail program through which you can exchange messages with others over the Internet. You can send a mail message to anyone for whom you have an address and you can receive messages in the Mail program.

Additionally, you can use the Internet Mail program to send files—such as reports, letters, spreadsheets, and so on—attached to a message to share with others.

In order to use Internet Mail, you must have a connection through an Internet Service Provider and a modem attached to your computer or over the network. See Appendix A for information about configuring your computer for the Internet.

OPENING AND CLOSING THE INTERNET MAIL PROGRAM

You can start the Internet Mail application from either the Internet Explorer or from the menus, as described below. Similar to Internet Explorer, exiting the program and disconnecting from the Internet are two separate procedures, as explained in this task.

To start the Internet Mail application, follow these steps:

1. Choose Start, Programs, Internet Mail. The Internet Mail window appears (see Figure 21.1).

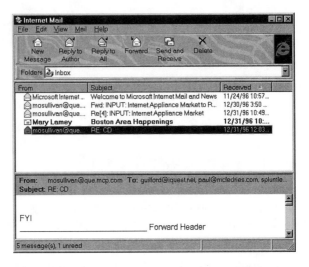

FIGURE 21.1 Send and receive mail over the Internet.

2. If you are not connected to the Internet, you can click the Send and Receive button on the toolbar to display the Connect To dialog box. For more information, see Appendix A.

Different Ways to Connect You can connect to the Internet from Internet Explorer (see Lesson 20) or from Internet News (see Lesson 22). While in the Explorer or News program, you can easily start the Internet Mail program and check your mail, send and receive messages, and so on, without closing the other application; then switch back and forth between the applications to take full advantage of the Internet.

---

3. Choose OK and the program dials your ISP and connects to the Internet. When connected, the program checks for new messages and sends any messages you may have written.

To disconnect from the Internet, follow these steps:

1. To exit the Internet Mail program, choose File, Exit.

2. Open the My Computer window and double-click the Dial-Up Networking icon. The Dial-Up Networking dialog box appears. Select your current connection and choose File, Disconnect. Close the open windows.

READING MAIL

The messages in your Inbox that are in bold type are messages that have not been read. Messages in regular type have been opened but remain in the Inbox until you either delete or move them to another folder.

To read a message, you can select it in the upper pane of the Internet Mail window and the message text is displayed on the lower pane. You also can double-click the message to open the window so you see the text in a better view (see Figure 21.2).

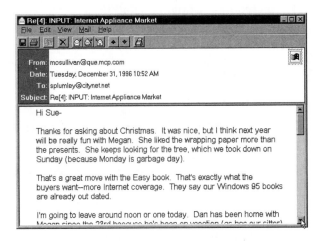

FIGURE 21.2 View the message in its own window.

Following are some other things you can do with open mail:

- To print an open message, choose File, Print.

- To delete a message, choose File, Delete.

- To close a message, choose File, Close.

- To read the next message in the list without closing the opened one, choose View, Next Message; to read the previous message, choose View, Previous Message.

REPLYING TO A MESSAGE

You can reply to any message you receive, and Internet Mail automatically places a copy of the original message in your reply, separated from your text by a short, dashed line and identified with the > symbol preceding each line of the original message, including headers. When you reply to a message, the application also addresses the message to the original author and uses the subject of the original message as the subject of the reply, but with an RE: preceding the original subject.

To reply to an open message, follow these steps:

1. In the open message to which you want to reply, choose Mail, Reply to Author.

> **Want to Make Multiple Replies?** If the original message was sent to more than one person (ie. carbon copies), you can send the reply to each person who originally received the message by choosing Mail, Reply to All.

2. In the Reply message window, add any names in the Cc area if you want to send a carbon copy of the message to someone else.

3. Enter the text of your message above the original text (see Figure 21.3).

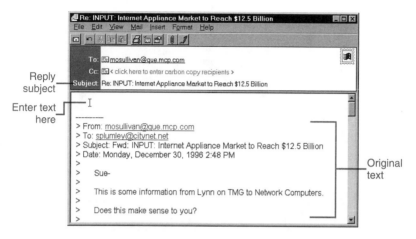

Reply subject

Enter text here

Original text

FIGURE 21.3   Reply to a message in Internet Mail.

4. When you're ready to send the message, choose File, Send Message or press Alt+S. If you're not connected to the Internet, Internet Mail stores your message in the Outbox and sends the message after you connect.

CREATING MAIL

You also can create a new message in Internet Mail. When you create a message, you'll need to know the recipient's Internet address. Then you add text as a subject and the message text. You send a new message the same way you send a reply.

To create a new mail message, follow these steps:

1. In Internet Mail, choose Mail, New Message; alternatively, click the New Message button.

2. In the New Message window, enter the address of the recipient in the To text box. Alternatively, click the address icon next to the To text box to display the Windows Address Book (see Figure 21.4).

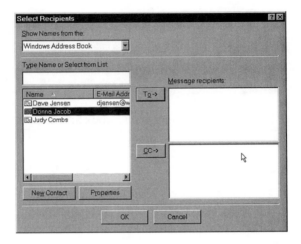

Figure 21.4 Use the address book to store addresses you often use.

3. If you want to add addresses to the address book, in the Select Recipients dialog box, click the New Contact button. Enter the name and e-mail address of the person in the Properties dialog box and the choose OK.

> **TIP**
>
> **Add More Info** You also can add information—such as a home phone number and address, business information, and notes—to the Properties dialog box about any recipient by clicking the various tabs and filling in the information.

4. To address the message to any person on your list, select the name and then click the To button; Internet Mail copies the name and address of that person to the To list box. You can add multiple names to the To list, or you can select any names and click the CC button to add them to the carbon copy list.

5. When you're done, click the OK button to return to the New Message window.

6. Click the Subject field and enter a topic for the message.

7. Click the message area and enter the text for your message.

8. Choose File, Send Message when you're ready to send the mail. If you're not connected to the Internet, Internet Mail stores your message in the Outbox and sends the message after you connect.

You can also do the following things before sending a message:

- To set a priority, or level of importance, for the message, choose Mail, Set Priority, and then choose either High, Normal, or Low. The default priority is Normal.

- To attach a file, choose Insert, File Attachment. In the Insert Attachment dialog box, select the file you want to attach and choose the Attach button. Internet Mail adds the file, represented by an icon, to your message.

- To format the message text, select the text and choose Format, Font or Format, Align. You also can create bulleted text in your message by selecting the text and choosing Format, Bullets.

In this lesson, you learned how to open and close the Internet Mail program, read and reply to mail, and create mail. In the next lesson, you learn to use Internet News.

USING INTERNET NEWS

In this lesson, you learn how to open and close the Internet News application in Windows, subscribe to a newsgroup, and download messages.

WHAT IS INTERNET NEWS?

Another Internet application included with Windows 95 is Internet News. With over 15,000 newsgroups on the Internet, you can use Internet News to exchange ideas and information about business, politics, hobbies, and many other interests. Usenet newsgroups (forums in which people exchange ideas on the Internet) enable you to contact others with similar, or completely different, ideas.

Newsgroup A collection of related messages about a topic which people have in common; for example, there is a computer consulting newsgroup, a dolphin newsgroup, an Irish music newsgroup, and so on.

Forum An area of the Internet that enables people to exchange ideas about a topic of interest.

You can pose questions about your new computer, or state opinions about the best type of dog to use in hunting grouse. Discuss your home decorating ideas or meet people who write science fiction short stories. There are literally thousands of forums you can search, read about, and visit time and again. The Windows' Internet News application enables you to browse a list of available Usenet groups, search groups for a topic or description, view a topic and related responses posted, and much more.

OPENING AND CLOSING THE INTERNET NEWS PROGRAM

When you open the Internet News program, Windows connects to the Internet. Initially, the program downloads a complete list of newsgroups.

To open and close the Internet News program, follow these steps:

1. Choose Start, Programs, Internet News. The Internet News dialog box appears.

   If this is the first time you've used the program or if you've not subscribed to a newsgroup before, a dialog box appears asking if you want to view a list of available newsgroups. Choose Yes to continue.

Long Download   Downloading an entire list of news groups may take some time; luckily, you only download the whole list once and then periodically add new lists to the current one.

   After you've subscribed to one or more newsgroups, the Connect To dialog box appears.

2. The Connect To dialog box appears. Choose OK to continue. Internet News dials your ISP and connects to the news server, downloading the available newsgroups for you.

How Do I Connect To?   You must set up your computer to access the Internet before you can attach to Internet News. See Appendix A for information.

3. The Newsgroups dialog box appears, listing all available newsgroups (see Figure 22.1). To view or subscribe to a newsgroup, see the next section.

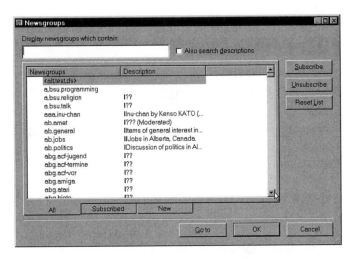

FIGURE 22.1   View the list of available newsgroups.

4. To exit the Internet News program, cancel the Newsgroup dialog box to return to the Internet News window. Choose File, Disconnect and then File, Close to close the program and disconnect from the news server.

The Modem is Still Connected!   If you're still connected to the Internet and want to disconnect, open the My Computer window and double-click the Dial-Up Networking icon. The Dial-Up Networking dialog box appears. Select your current connection and choose File, Disconnect. Close the open windows.

VIEWING AND SUBSCRIBING TO A NEWSGROUP

You can view a list of current newsgroups at any time and subscribe to those you want to become a member of. When you view the newsgroup's messages, you can read those messages and respond to them. When you subscribe to a newsgroup, you simply make it easier to find the forum again when you connect.

To view the list of newsgroups in the Newsgroups window at any time, choose News, Newsgroups in the Internet News window or click the Newsgroups button. Scroll through the list of newsgroups to see what groups are available.

So Many Newsgroups, So Little Time If you want to search for a specific newsgroup or topic, enter the topic in the Display Newsgroups Which Contain text box within the Newsgroups dialog box and wait just a second or two (do not press Enter). Internet Mail lists any newsgroups containing the topic you entered.

To view a newsgroups' messages and subscribe to a group, follow these steps:

1. In the Newsgroups dialog box, select the newsgroup whose messages you want to view.

2. Choose the Go To button near the bottom of the dialog box. Internet News lists the subjects of the messages in the Internet News window, as shown in figure 22.2. To learn how to read and reply to messages, see the next section.

3. To subscribe to a newsgroup, in the Internet News window after selecting a newsgroup and viewing its messages, choose News, Newsgroups. The Newsgroup dialog box appears. Alternatively, if you're already in the Newsgroups dialog box, go on to step 4.

4. Select the newsgroup you want to subscribe to in the list of Newsgroups. Click the Subscribe button to the right of the list. An icon appears next to the newsgroup. Subscribe to multiple newsgroups, if you want. When you're done, click OK.

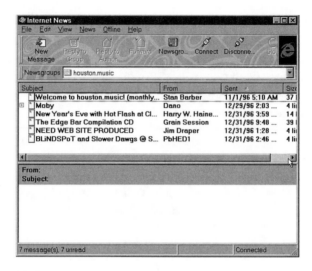

FIGURE 22.2 Scroll through the messages of any newsgroups.

You can view, in the Newsgroups dialog box, only those groups to which you've subscribed by clicking the Subscribed button located at the bottom of the Newsgroups list. You can, alternatively, click the New button to view only new newsgroups or click the All button to view all newsgroups.

READING AND POSTING MESSAGES

After you find a newsgroup in which you're interested, you can read the messages and post your own message at any time, if you want. Reading and posting messages is like talking to others about your similar interests.

Posting When you post a message, you're simply creating a message to send to the group or to reply to the author of a message you read, just as you would with e-mail. See Lesson 21 for more information.

To read and post messages in a newsgroup, follow these steps:

1. To read a message in the Internet News window, double-click the message in the upper pane. The message appears in a message window (see Figure 22.3).

Easier to Read Message   If you select any message subject, its text appears in the lower pane of the Internet News window; however, if you double-click the subject to open the message window, it's easier to read and reply to the message.

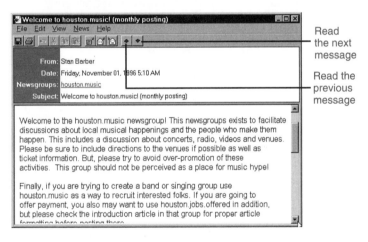

Read the next message

Read the previous message

FIGURE 22.3   Open and read the messages in the forum.

2. You can continue to read messages from this same window by clicking either the Previous button or the Next button in the toolbar.

3. If you want to reply to a message, choose News, Reply to Newsgroup. The Reply message window appears with a copy of the original message and the message's topic in the Subject area of the header.

4. Enter your reply and choose File, Post Message to send it to the newsgroup.

To compose a new message to the group, choose News, New Message to Newsgroup. Complete the message as you would any e-mail message, by entering the newsgroup's address (you can get it from the Newsgroups dialog box), the subject, and the text. Choose File, Post Message to send it.

DOWNLOADING MESSAGES

If you want, you can download the messages from a group so you can read and respond to them offline. Later, when you connect to the Internet again, you can send your replies to the group. You might want to download messages to save on your phone bill or your connect time, if your ISP limits your access to the Internet.

You can mark one message, all messages, or a thread for downloading.

Mark   Marking a message is attaching a tag or label to it to indicate you want to save, download, read, or otherwise denote the message.

Thread   A group of messages and replies about a specific topic within the newsgroup.

Download   Copying message(s) to your computer's hard drive for use offline.

To download messages, follow these steps:

1. To mark one message for download, select the message in the Internet News window and choose Offline, Mark Message for Download.

To mark a thread, select the message with a plus sign (+) in front of it in the upper pane of the Internet News window and choose Offline, Mark Thread for Download.

To mark all messages, choose Offline, Mark All for Download.

2. Choose Offline, Post and Download and Internet News to download the marked messages.

In this lesson, you learned how to open and close the Internet News application in Windows, subscribe to a newsgroup, and download messages. In the next lesson, you learn to work with Multimedia.

23 WORKING WITH MULTIMEDIA

In this lesson, you learn how to use the CD player, Media Player, and ActiveMovie.

USING THE CD PLAYER

You can use your CD-ROM drive on your computer to play music CDs. You must have a sound card installed and you may or may not use external speakers with your computer. With the CD Player, you can play CDs, switch the order in which you play tracks, and select specific tracks to play.

To use the CD Player, follow these steps:

1. Choose Start, Programs, Accessories, and Multimedia. From the Multimedia menu, choose CD Player. The CD Player appears; if you have a data CD or no CD in the CD-ROM drive, you'll see the message "Date or no disc loaded" (see Figure 23.1).

Still Won't Recognize the CD? If you insert a CD and your CD player still does not recognize it, you'll need to make sure you have a sound card installed in your computer and that you have a Windows 95 driver for the sound card installed. Double-click the System icon in the Control Panel and select the Device Manager tab. Double-click the Sound, video, and game controllers device type to see if there is an installed sound card. If you see a yellow circle with an exclamation point in it or no sound card listed, you have a problem.

Play   Pause

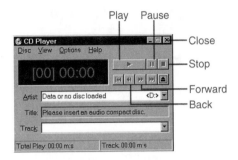

FIGURE 23.1   Use the CD Player to play music CDs from your computer.

2. Insert the CD. Click the Play button to play, the Pause button to temporarily stop the CD, and use the Stop button to stop the music.

3. To change the order of the tracks that play, as opposed to playing the tracks in the order they fall on the CD, choose Options, Random Order.

TIP   **Not Loud Enough?**   To adjust the volume of the CD Player, choose View, Volume Control. The Volume Control application appears—use it to adjust the volume.

USING THE MEDIA PLAYER

Use the Media Player to play audio, video, and animation files in Windows 95. You can play a multimedia file, rewind the file, and fast forward the file. You also can copy a multimedia file into a document that you or someone else can play back. Video for Windows files have an AVI extension.

To open and use the Media Player, follow these steps:

1. Choose Start, Programs, Accesories, Multimedia, and then select Media Player. The Media Player opens (see Figure 23.2).

FIGURE 23.2   Play video and animation files with the Media Player.

2. From the Device menu, select the device type you want to play: ActiveMovie (animation), Video for Windows, or CD audio.

3. If you choose the ActiveMovie or Video for Windows option, an Open dialog box appears from which you can locate and choose the file you want to play. If you choose the CD audio option, then choose File, Open to select the file you want.

4. Choose the Play button to play the file.

USING ACTIVEMOVIE

The ActiveMovie player is similar to the Media Player; you can play animated clips or movies on both applications. Files you play using the ActiveMovie Control box include the following types: MPEG, MPE, MPG, MPA, ENC, and DAT. These extensions represent various file types of movies or animations that have been compressed somewhat because of their very large size.

To use the ActiveMovie program, follow these steps:

1. Choose Start, Programs, Accessories, Multimedia, and then choose ActiveMovie Control. The Open dialog box appears.

2. Choose the file you want to play and then click the Open button.

3. As the file plays, you can control the movie from the ActiveMovie Control box (see Figure 23.3).

FIGURE 23.3 Choose to play or stop the animation using the ActiveMovie Control box.

USING A MULTIMEDIA FILE IN A DOCUMENT

You can place any multimedia file in a document so you or someone else can play the file at any time from within the document. You can copy the multimedia file and then paste it into the document.

To use a multimedia file in a document, follow these steps:

1. In the Media Player, open the File menu and choose Open.

2. Double-click the file you want to copy.

3. Choose Edit, Options and specify the options you want.

4. Open the document to which you want to paste the file and position the insertion point.

5. Choose Edit, Paste.

To play back a multimedia file from within a document, you double-click the icon representing the file.

In this lesson, you learned how to use the CD player, Media player, and ActiveMovie. In the next lesson, you learn about customizing the appearance of Windows 95.

CUSTOMIZING THE APPEARANCE OF WINDOWS 95

In this lesson, you learn how to change the color scheme, add wallpaper to the desktop, and use a screen saver.

OPENING THE CONTROL PANEL

You use the Control Panel to control such aspects of Windows as the colors, fonts, modems, sounds, and so on. Figure 24.1 shows the Control Panel window; some of your icons may differ from those in this figure.

FIGURE 24.1 Control your sounds, colors, hardware, and so on using the Control Panel icons.

To open the Control Panel, follow these steps:

1. Choose the Start button.

2. Select the Settings menu, Control Panel. To open any icon in the Control Panel, double-click that icon.

CHANGING THE COLOR SCHEME

You can change the color scheme that Windows uses for your desktop, windows, menus, title bars, and so on, to a preset color scheme. To change the Windows color scheme, follow these steps:

1. In the Control Panel, open the Display icon by double-clicking it.

2. Choose the Appearance tab. Figure 24.2 shows the Display Properties dialog box with the Appearance tab displayed.

FIGURE 24.2   Use the tabs in the Display Properties dialog box to control the features pertaining to the desktop.

3. From the Scheme drop-down list, select a color scheme. The sample at the top of the dialog box shows what the new colors in the windows and desktop will look like.

4. Check out as many different color schemes as you want. When you're satisfied with the selected color scheme, click OK. If you plan to make other changes to the Display Properties dialog box (in other tabs), choose the Apply button to accept the changes made to the Appearance tab and continue.

 TIP   **Default Colors**   If you want to go back to the scheme originally on your computer, choose Windows Standard.

Adding Wallpaper and Patterns

You can choose from a variety of designs to apply to your desktop using the Display icon in the Control Panel. Figure 24.3 shows the Background tab of the Display Properties dialog box and its options.

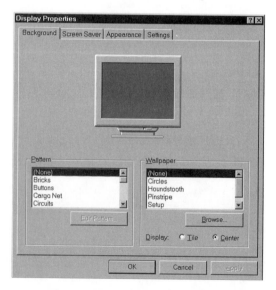

Figure 24.3   Use the Background tab to add wallpaper or patterns to your desktop.

ADDING WALLPAPER

Wallpaper consists of colorful, bitmapped images that you can display on your desktop for decoration.

Bitmapped images   Bitmap is a file type used for storing images. Because the image is stored as a series of dots, called pixels, the image has rough edges and shows few details.

To apply a wallpaper design to your desktop, follow these steps:

1. In the Display Properties dialog box, choose the Background tab.

2. In the Wallpaper section, scroll the list and select the wallpaper design you want to use.

3. Click the Center option button to have Windows center one small icon from the file in the center of the desktop screen. Click the Tile option button to have Windows repeat the wallpaper icon so that the entire desktop is filled with the pattern.

4. Choose OK to close the dialog box and accept the wallpaper design. Alternatively, click the apply button to accept this change and continue making changes to the other tabs in the dialog box.

Why So Slow?   If you notice that your computer reacts more slowly than it did before, that's because using wallpaper and/or patterns for your desktop requires extra memory. If you're low on memory, you may want to use only a solid color for your desktop.

ADDING PATTERNS

Patterns are additional designs you can apply to your desktop for decoration. To apply a pattern, follow these steps:

1. In the Display Properties dialog box, choose the Background tab.

2. In the Pattern area of the dialog box, scroll the list and choose the pattern you want to use.

3. **(Optional)** Choose the Edit Pattern button and change the pattern by clicking the mouse in the pattern box. As you add to the design, the Sample box changes to reflect your additions. To remove an addition, click the box a second time. Choose Change to accept the changes and Done to close the Edit Pattern dialog box. If you do not want to save your changes, choose Done and when prompted to save, choose No.

4. Choose OK to close the Display Properties dialog box. The pattern appears on your desktop.

You Can't Use Both   If you select both a pattern and a wallpaper in the Desktop dialog box, the wallpaper overlays the pattern.

ADDING A SCREEN SAVER

Even though screen savers are no longer needed to prevent damage to your monitor from burn-in, they're still fun to use. If you select a screen saver, Windows runs a pattern across your screen anytime your computer is inactive for the specified length of time. To return to the screen and continue working, you simply press a key or move the mouse.

Burn-in In older monitors, extremely light screens (such as those you see in Windows) had what is called a burn-in effect. When a Windows screen was left on the computer for a long period of time, the Windows image burned into the monitor. Then when the monitor was turned off or used in DOS, a ghost of the Windows screen remained. Screen savers were originally used to keep the burn-in effect from ruining monitors. Newer monitors have built-in protection against burn-in.

To select a screen saver, follow these steps:

1. In the Display Properties dialog box, choose the Screen Saver tab. Figure 24.4 shows the Screen Saver tab of the Display Properties dialog box.

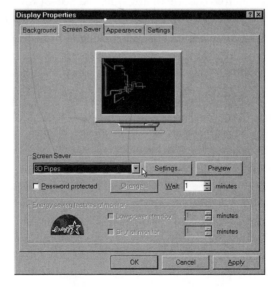

FIGURE 24.4 Change screen savers periodically, just for fun.

2. In the Screen Saver section, open the drop-down list and choose a screen saver.

3. Click the Preview button to view a sample of the screen saver. When you finish viewing the screen saver, click the mouse button to return to the Display Properties dialog box.

4. In the Wait text box, enter the number of minutes you want Windows to wait for your computer to be inactive before it starts the screen saver.

5. **(Optional)** Choose Password protected if you want your screen saver to remain on-screen until you enter your password. This prevents other individual from viewing your screen without your knowledge.

6. **(Optional)** Choose the Settings button to set any specific options that deal with your selected screen saver. Then choose OK to close the Settings dialog box.

7. Choose OK to close the dialog box and accept the changes. The next time you leave your computer inactive for the specified amount of time, the screen saver you selected appears on your screen.

In this lesson, you learned how to change the color scheme, add wallpaper to the desktop, and use a screen saver. In the next lesson, you learn to control hardware settings.

CONTROLLING HARDWARE SETTINGS

In this lesson, you learn how to change the date and time setting on your computer, modify mouse settings, and configure your modem.

ALTERING THE DATE AND TIME

You use the Control Panel to set your computer's system date and time, which is used to time-stamp files as you create and modify them. In addition, many applications allow you to automatically insert the date and time on-screen or when you print, so you'll want to be sure to have the right time on your computer.

 Bad Battery? If you set your time and date and then find that the date is wrong when you start your computer again, you probably have a bad battery. Check your computer's documentation for instructions on how to replace the battery.

To check or set the date and time, follow these steps:

1. From the Desktop, choose Start, Settings, and Control Panel.

2. In the Control Panel window, double-click the Date/Time icon. The Date/Time Properties dialog box appears with the Date & Time tab selected (see Figure 25.1).

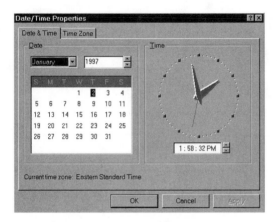

Figure 25.1   The Date/Time Properties dialog box enables you to set the date and/or time on your computer.

3. In the Date area, select the correct month and year from the drop-down lists; then click the day on the calendar.

4. To change the time, click the portion of the time you want to change and either enter the correct number or use the spinner arrows to increase or decrease the value accordingly.

5. **(Optional)** Choose the Time Zone tab and check the Automatically Adjust Clock for Daylight Savings Changes check box (put a check mark in it) if you want Windows to change the time automatically in the spring and fall.

6. Select OK or press Enter to accept the changes you have made.

Time Zone If necessary, use the Time Zone drop-down list to change your current time zone. You might use this option if you move or travel with your computer.

MODIFYING MOUSE SETTINGS

The mouse settings enable you to change tracking, to choose a double-click speed, and to swap the left and right mouse buttons. Figure 25.2 shows the Mouse Properties dialog box.

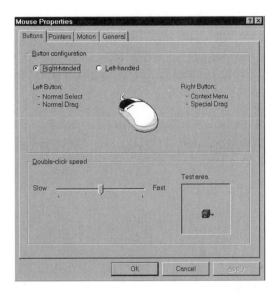

FIGURE 25.2   Adjust mouse settings to better suit your needs.

By double-clicking the Mouse icon in the Control Panel, you access the Mouse Properties dialog box, where you can modify the following settings for your mouse:

- **Pointer Speed (Motion tab)**   Use pointer speed when you're working on a notebook or laptop computer. The speed adjusts the rate at which the pointer travels across the screen, making it easier to find your pointer on the small screen. Set the speed to Slow if you have trouble seeing the mouse pointer; set the speed to Fast if the "slow-motion" mouse is distracting.

- **Pointer Trail (Motion tab)**   If you use a notebook or laptop computer, you can choose to display a trail, or echo the pointer, to help you find the pointer on a small, poor-resolution screen. Choose Short for a brief trail or Long for an extended trail.

- **Double-Click Speed (Buttons tab)**   Adjust the speed to suit your finger's double-click speed. Slower means you can actually perform the two clicks more slowly. Adjust the speed and then test in the Text area.

- **Swap Left/Right Buttons (Buttons tab)**   Check this box to switch buttons, if you're left-handed or just more comfortable with the switch.

To modify the mouse settings, follow these steps:

1. From the Desktop, choose Start, Settings, Control Panel.

2. In the Control Panel, double-click the Mouse icon to open the Mouse Properties dialog box.

3. Adjust the settings.

4. Choose OK to accept the changes you have made.

Configuring the Modem

If you have a modem attached to your computer, you can modify the settings. Additionally, you can add or remove modems easily using the Modem Wizard.

Adding a Modem

Before adding a modem, connect the modem to your machine. If it's external, turn it on. If you've added an internal modem, make sure it's properly connected and that the computer's case is closed before turning your computer on.

To add a modem, follow these steps:

1. From the Desktop, choose Start, Settings, Control Panel.

2. Double-click the Modem icon to open the Modems Properties dialog box (see Figure 25.3).

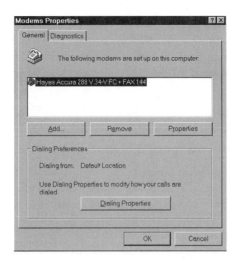

FIGURE 25.3   Configure your modem in the Modems Properties dialog box.

3. To add a new modem, choose the Add button. The Install New Modem dialog box appears, as shown in Figure 25.4.

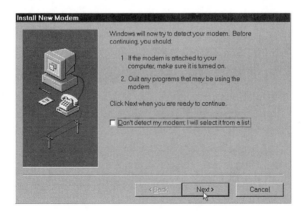

FIGURE 25.4   Adding a modem is as easy as following the directions.

4. Let Windows detect your modem by choosing the Next button; then follow the directions on-screen to complete the installation.

When Windows returns to the Modems Properties dialog box, you can configure the dialing properties, as described in the next section, or you can choose the Close button to return to the Desktop.

 TIP **Too Many Modems?**   To remove a modem you no longer use, open the Modems Properties dialog box and select the modem from the list. Choose the Remove button. Choose Close to return to the Desktop.

Modifying Dialing Properties

Dialing properties control how your calls are dialed. You may never need to modify these properties; however, if you're using a notebook and you use your modem from the road, hotels, and so on, you'll want to change dialing properties when you change locations.

To modify dialing properties, follow these steps:

1. In the Modems Properties dialog box, choose the Dialing Properties button on the General tab. The Dialing Properties dialog box appears with the My Locations tab showing (see Figure 25.5).

2. In the Where I Am area of the dialog box, enter the area code and choose the country from which you are calling.

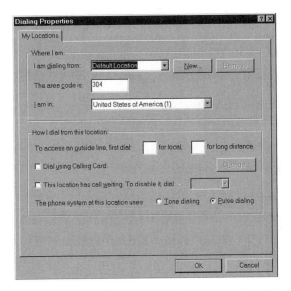

FIGURE 25.5   Use the dialing properties when you go on the road with your computer.

3. In the How I Dial From This Location area, enter the following information, as required:

- **To Access an Outside Line, First Dial**   If you must dial a number to access an outside line, as is often required at hotels or offices, enter that number in this area. Note you can enter a number to dial to access a local and/or long distance line.

- **Dial Using Calling Card**   Select the check box and the choose the Change button to enter your calling card number.

- **This Location Has Call Waiting**   If the location has call waiting, enter the code to disable that feature while you're calling with the modem.

- **The Phone System at This Location Uses:** Choose either Tone or Pulse dialing.

4. If this is a location you often make modem calls from, you can save these settings for the next time you need to make a call. At the top of the dialog box, choose the New button. The text in the I Am Dialing From text box becomes selected; enter the location name to save it, such as **Dartmouth Hotel** or **Bill's Office**. Press Enter to accept the changes and close the dialog box.

5. Choose OK to accept the changes and close the Modem Properties dialog box.

Changing Modem Properties

You also can modify certain modem settings such as port, speed, and connection from the Modems Properties dialog box. The contents of a Modems Properties dialog box depends on the type and model of the modem, but generally, you'll find settings for such properties as port, speaker volume, maximum speed, and connection preferences.

To change your modem's properties, follow these steps:

1. In the Modems Properties dialog box, select the modem you are configuring from the list so the modem's name is highlighted.

2. Choose the Properties button. Make any changes in the dialog box according to your modem manufacturer's directions. If you have any questions about your modem's configuration, see the documentation that came with your modem.

3. Choose OK when finished setting the modem's properties. Choose Close to exit the Modems Properties dialog box.

In this lesson, you learned how to change the date and time setting on your computer, modify mouse settings, and configure your modem. In the next lesson, you learn to scan and defragment your disk.

ADVANCED DISK MANAGEMENT

*In this lesson, you learn how to scan
a disk for errors and how to
defragment a disk.*

SCANNING YOUR DISK

Windows includes a utility that enables you to scan a disk for
errors and then fix those errors. You use ScanDisk as a Windows
95 replacement for the old check disk (CHKDSK) command you
used in DOS. You can use ScanDisk on hard or floppy drives.

Errors normally take place, for example, when you exit Windows
by shutting off the computer or pressing **Ctrl+Alt+Del** instead of
shutting down properly.

To scan your disk for errors, follow these steps:

1. Choose Start, Programs, Accessories, System Tools, and
   then choose ScanDisk.

2. In the ScanDisk dialog box, select the drive you want to
   scan (see Figure 26.1).

3. Choose the Standard type of test first, since it will generally notify you of most common errors. The Thorough
   test takes much longer to run.

4. Choose the Start button. Scandisk scans the disk and if it
   finds errors, notifies you of the error type and suggests
   solutions to the problem (see Figure 26.2).

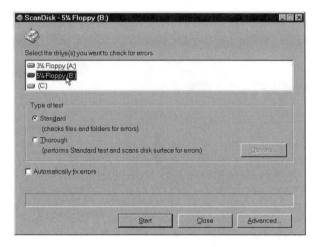

FIGURE 26.1   Scan a disk to make sure it has no errors or problems.

Don't Automatically Fix Errors   Even though Windows includes a check box enabling Scandisk to automatically fix errors, you shouldn't use this option so that you can examine each error yourself before fixing; sometimes smaller errors are a symtom of larger problems.

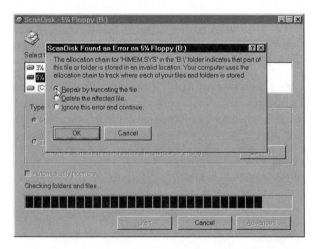

FIGURE 26.2   Choose an option for dealing with the error.

5. When ScanDisk is finished, it displays the results of the scan (see Figure 26.3).

FIGURE 26.3   Read the results of the disk scan.

6. Choose Close to exit the dialog box and return to the ScanDisk program. Choose Close to close ScanDisk.

DEFRAGMENTING YOUR DISK

A disk (hard or floppy) gets fragmented after you use it for an extended period of time, by the normal procedures of copying, cutting, deleting, and creating files. A disk is fragmented when one file is stored in several different sectors across a disk instead of one sector, all together. A fragmented file takes longer to access and save and a fragmented disk is not as efficient as one that is not fragmented.

Don't Worry Windows will not defragment your disk if it doesn't need it. Instead, the Defrag program will display a dialog box telling you it's not necessary to defragment at this time.

To defragment a disk, follow these steps:

1. Choose Start, Programs, Accessories, System Tools, and then Disk Defragmenter.

2. In the Select Drive dialog box, choose the drive you want to defragment; you can defragment a hard or floppy drive. Choose OK.

3. Defrag begins to defragment the disk, showing a progress bar as it works. When finished, the Disk Defragmenter displays a dialog box telling you it is done. Choose Yes to quit the program or No to defragment another disk (see Figure 26.4).

Figure 26.4   Defrag notifies you when it's done.

    Taking a Long Time?   The more fragmented a drive is, the longer it takes to defragment it. If you want, you can click the Show Details in the Disk Defragmenter progress dialog box to view the process as it takes place.

In this lesson, you learned how to scan a disk for errors and to defragment a disk.

CONFIGURING FOR THE INTERNET

You must have an Internet connection before you can use Internet Explorer, Internet Mail, or Internet News. Windows makes it easy for you to configure your Internet connection. But first you'll need to get an Internet Service Provider (ISP) that is located in your area. An ISP provides you with all of the information—IP address, subnet mask, host name, and so on—you need to configure Windows 95 for the Internet.

After you set up your computer for using Internet Explorer, you can explore Web pages, send and receive e-mail, and access news groups on the Internet. Windows makes it easy to set up for using the Internet by providing a Wizard that guides you through the steps.

This appendix shows you how to connect to the Internet and then how to use the three Internet applications: Internet Explorer, Internet Mail, and Internet News.

To set up for the Internet, follow these steps:

1. Choose Programs, Accessories, Internet Tools and from this menu, select Get on the Internet. The Internet Connection Wizard appears. Choose the Next button to start the process.

2. Choose the **Manual** option if you have an account with a ISP and want to set up your computer with addresses and information your ISP has provided. Click the **Next** button to continue to set up. If you chose Manual, an introductory screen appears; choose Next.

TIP   **Automatic for ISP**   If you do not have an ISP and you want Windows to find an ISP for you, choose Automatic and follow the directions on-screen in the Wizard dialog boxes that follow.

3. The How to Connect Wizard box appears. Select the method you'll use to connect to the Internet. You'll most likely use the phone line to connect; however, if you're a member of a network, choose the LAN option instead. These instructions assume you're using a phone line. Click Next.

4. The Wizard next asks if you want to use Internet Mail; choose Yes and click the Next button. If you do not set up Internet Mail, you won't be able to send or receive e-mail messages over the Internet using Windows' Internet mail application; however, you could use a third-party mail program such as Eudora.

5. The Installing Files Wizard dialog box appears. Click Next to continue the process. Windows may prompt you for your Windows CD-ROM; insert the disk and choose OK to continue.

6. When Windows is done copying files, it displays the Service Provider Information Wizard dialog box. Enter the name of your ISP and choose Next.

7. In the Phone Number Wizard dialog box, enter the area code (if applicable) and the phone number of your ISP. Choose the country code, if different from the US. Click the Next button.

8. In the User Name and Password Wizard dialog box, enter the User name and password assigned to you by your ISP. Notice the password enters as asterisks instead of characters, to protect your privacy. Click Next.

9. In the IP Address dialog box, choose the appropriate response and click the Next button. Your ISP may provide

your IP address automatically through a special server, called a DHCP server; however, make sure you check with the ISP first before choosing that option. Generally, you enter an IP address that your ISP assigns you in this Wizard box.

10. In the DNS Server Address Wizard dialog box, enter the number(s) or name(s) for the name server(s) your ISP uses. This information, as well as all other you use in the wizard, should be obtained from your ISP. Click Next.

11. If you're configuring for Internet Mail, enter your e-mail address and your ISP's Internet mail server in the Internet Mail Wizard dialog box. Click the Next button.

12. The Complete Configuration Wizard dialog box appears to let you know that set up is complete. Click the Finish button. When you click The Internet icon on the desktop, the connection you just created will appear.

INDEX

Complete and Return this Card
for a *FREE* Computer Book Catalog

Thank you for purchasing this book! You have purchased a
superior computer book written expressly for your needs. To
continue to provide the kind of up-to-date, pertinent coverage
you've come to expect from us, we need to hear from you.
Please take a minute to complete and return this self-addressed,
postage-paid form. In return, we'll send you a free catalog of all
our computer books on topics ranging from word processing to
programming and the internet.

☐   Mrs. ☐   Ms. ☐   Dr. ☐

ie (first) ☐☐☐☐☐☐☐☐☐   (M.I.) ☐   (last) ☐☐☐☐☐☐☐☐☐☐☐☐☐

cress ☐☐☐☐☐☐☐☐☐☐☐☐☐☐☐☐☐☐☐☐☐☐☐

☐☐☐☐☐☐☐☐☐☐☐☐☐☐☐☐☐☐☐☐☐☐☐

☐☐☐☐☐☐☐☐☐☐☐ State ☐☐   Zip ☐☐☐☐☐ ☐☐☐☐

ie ☐☐☐   ☐☐☐   ☐☐☐☐   Fax   ☐☐☐   ☐☐☐☐

ipany Name ☐☐☐☐☐☐☐☐☐☐☐☐☐☐☐☐☐☐☐☐☐☐☐

iail address ☐☐☐☐☐☐☐☐☐☐☐☐☐☐☐☐☐☐☐☐☐☐☐☐☐☐☐

Please check at least (3) influencing factors for purchasing this book.

nt or back cover information on book .... ☐
ccial approach to the content .... ☐
mpleteness of content .... ☐
thor's reputation .... ☐
olisher's reputation .... ☐
ok cover design or layout .... ☐
ex or table of contents of book .... ☐
ce of book .... ☐
ccial effects, graphics, illustrations .... ☐
ier (Please specify): _____ ☐

How did you first learn about this book?

rnet Site .... ☐
v in Macmillan Computer
Publishing catalog .... ☐
commended by store personnel .... ☐
v the book on bookshelf at store .... ☐
commended by a friend .... ☐
ceived advertisement in the mail .... ☐
v an advertisement in: _____ ☐
id book review in: _____ ☐
ier (Please specify): _____ ☐

How many computer books have you purchased in the last six months?

s book only .... ☐   3 to 5 books .... ☐
ooks .... ☐   More than 5 .... ☐

4. Where did you purchase this book?

Bookstore .... ☐
Computer Store .... ☐
Consumer Electronics Store .... ☐
Department Store .... ☐
Office Club .... ☐
Warehouse Club .... ☐
Mail Order .... ☐
Direct from Publisher .... ☐
Internet site .... ☐
Other (Please specify): .... ☐

5. How long have you been using a computer?

Less than 6 months .. ☐   6 months to a year ..... ☐
1 to 3 years .... ☐   More than 3 years ...... ☐

6. What is your level of experience with personal computers and with the subject of this book?

	With PC's	With subject of book
New	☐	☐
Casual	☐	☐
Accomplished	☐	☐
Expert	☐	☐

Source Code—ISBN: 0-7897-1160-5

7. Which of the following best describes your job title?

Administrative Assistant .... ☐
Coordinator .... ☐
Manager/Supervisor .... ☐
Director .... ☐
Vice President .... ☐
President/CEO/COO .... ☐
Lawyer/Doctor/Medical Professional ..... ☐
Teacher/Educator/Trainer .... ☐
Engineer/Technician .... ☐
Consultant .... ☐
Not employed/Student/Retired .... ☐
Other (Please specify): .... ☐

8. Which of the following best describes the area of the company your job title falls under?

Accounting .... ☐
Engineering .... ☐
Manufacturing .... ☐
Marketing .... ☐
Operations .... ☐
Sales .... ☐
Other (Please specify): .... ☐

9. What is your age?

Under 20 .... ☐
21-29 .... ☐
30-39 .... ☐
40-49 .... ☐
50-59 .... ☐
60-over .... ☐

10. Are you:

Male .... ☐
Female .... ☐

11. Which computer publications do you read regularly? (Please list)

_____
_____
_____
_____
_____
_____
_____
_____
_____

Comments: _____
_____
_____

Fold here and scotch-tape

> ‖‖·‖·‖·‖·‖·‖···‖·‖·‖·‖·‖···‖‖‖···‖‖·‖·‖